# Growing up in
# WARTIME
# SOUTHAMPTON

The author's seaman's discharge book. Taken a the end of his course at the National Sea Training School Sharpness in March 1957. (Photo courtesy of The National Archives at Kew, London)

# Growing up in
# WARTIME
# SOUTHAMPTON

## Someone Else's Trousers

JAMES MARSH

*This book is dedicated to my son James, his lovely partner Sarah,*
*and my grandson Jayden.*

*Thanks for all the love and support.*

First published 2011

The History Press
The Mill, Brimscombe Port
Stroud, Gloucestershire, GL5 2QG
www.thehistorypress.co.uk

British Library Cataloguing in Publication Data.
A catalogue record for this book is available from the British Library.

ISBN 978 0 7524 5840 3

Typesetting and origination by The History Press
Printed in Malta

# CONTENTS

# Foreword

This book is, essentially, a voyage of discovery. In the space of a few short years, the author discovered that there was a way of life that did not involve air-raid sirens and bombs. He found that there was an important man in his family's life – his father – and that the world extended beyond the borders of Belgrave Road, Portswood and Southampton. In the process he grew up, and it is this story, which is so touchingly, and often hilariously, portrayed within these pages.

If you visit Belgrave Road today it is unrecognisable as a street of terraced houses, teeming with life. It is now a busy industrial estate, the houses long gone. This is a pity, for with them went a slice of Southampton's history. It is for this reason that this memoir is so important: Not only does it document the events of one man's life, it also saves for posterity a world that no longer exists.

I hope you enjoy this book as much as I have done. Happy reading!

*Penny Legg, 2011*

# *Acknowledgements*

My thanks go to the following:

My son James for all his work editing the manuscript; Penny and Joe Legg for their valuable help and friendship; Nicola Guy from The History Press; Sue Woolgar and the staff of Southampton Archives department for their help; The Ford family of No.4 Belgrave Road for permission to use the VE-Day photographs; My aunt Vicky for her contribution to the story; My sisters Sue, Pat and Jean, and my brothers George and Ron for their memories; Former residents of Belgrave Road with whom I grew up; John F. Hunt Demolition Co. for their expert advice about demolition in the 1960s; Dyer Brothers boatyard in Southampton for their help and co-operation; St Denys' Rowing and Sailing Club for the photographs of the rowing boats as they are today; The owner and staff of Caroline's T-shirts.

Cover image courtesy of Southampton Constabulary History Society.

# Introduction

This is a story of two worlds that are far removed from one another. I was born during the first year of the Second World War and my infancy was spent in air-raid shelters outside our home. Bombs constantly rained down from the German Luftwaffe, as they tried to destroy the city of Southampton.

I was nearly five years old when I first met my father after his demob from the commandos. He appeared in our home suddenly, and we now had to get to know this man we knew nothing about. I chronicle how we as a family coped with the post-war years, where rationing and shortages were a way of life. This was true not just for us but every family in our circumstances.

School life in the forties and fifties was very different from today. Nobody had television; we listened to programmes on radio. There were no calculators, mobile phones, computers and, in most cases, NO cars. We became proficient at producing homemade toys, bikes and trolleys. Life was always a challenge, but it was met by everyone with determination and sometimes miracles.

Many great occupations sadly no longer exist, or have changed beyond recognition, and I was fortunate enough to experience one. After hard training at the *Vindicatrix* Sea School I gained my discharge book and went to sea in Britain's Merchant Navy.

I also pay tribute to the brave men, my father included, who made up Six Troop Six Commando. These remarkable men, many of whom survive today, did so much to ensure this country's freedom from Nazi rule. I proudly include them in this book.

*James Marsh, 2011*

# 1

# *Grab the Black Bag*

We were all there in that black bag that hung on a hook behind the scullery door of No. 94 Belgrave Road. Birth certificates, the all important ration books, insurance policies, identity cards, in fact all things relevant to our existence were kept there. That bag was of paramount importance and had to be taken to the shelter every time we went. This was almost every night because by the time I entered the world, on 6 December 1940, the Second World War had already been raging for just over a year.

Air raids were now common, happening with horrifying and gruelling regularity. Each night was an awful lottery; no-one knew whether their home would still be standing, or whether it had been reduced to rubble by one of the many bombs that fell on Southampton from late 1940 onwards. Records show this amounted to 2,569 high explosive bombs, 36 parachute mines and an estimated 32,000 incendiaries. The Blitz they called it and a blitz it was.

I was born in the maternity unit of Southampton's Borough Hospital (now Southampton General) in between two raids on the town, and from that clamorous start I was to know nearly five years of war. Indeed, on the night before my birth Southampton suffered one of its heaviest raids. My mother had to wait several hours for essential things like hot water and food because the hospital's facilities had all been knocked out by bomb damage. Like many other babies, I looked out at the world from the bottom drawer of my mother's sideboard. There were no carry cots in those days, so babies were simply wrapped in a shawl and placed there.

My earliest memories are of being at home in Belgrave Road with my mother, Mrs Edith Ann Marsh, my two sisters, Sue and Pat, and my brother George. Also living with us was a lady who literally saved my life early in 1942 after a serious accident. Her name was Mrs Spender and she rented two rooms. It was she who shepherded the children out when the siren sounded, and saw them safely to the shelter; she was always on hand in any crisis.

Number 94 Belgrave Road was one of five terraced houses that had been built later than the others on the street. The majority dated back to Victorian times, as did Belgrave Road itself when it had a tough reputation; so tough it was always said that police officers would only walk through in twos.

Ours was a three-bedroom house, only two of which were available to us as Mrs Spender occupied the other. The sleeping arrangements were quite simple; I, as the youngest, was in the front bedroom with my mother while Sue, Pat and George shared the small front room next door. The large rear bedroom that looked out over the garden was Mrs Spender's and, as such, was out of bounds to us. But not to a steady stream of mysterious men who came and went all the time. They were introduced as uncles or friends of hers who were just visiting. Three of these were brothers who lived a few doors away in Belgrave Road. We got to know them very well indeed, as their visits to Mrs Spender were regular.

There was one other room on the top floor, right by the stairs. To have a bathroom was almost unknown in Southampton at that time. The antiquated water heater, known as a geyser, produced an enormous explosion every time the gas ignited, frightening the life out of us. It may have only come out at a trickle but we did have hot running water. There the luxury ended however, because like everyone else in the road we had to use an outdoor toilet. This was situated just beyond the back door, across a concrete square. Beyond that our garden stretched away into the distance towards the fence that divided us from the railway. At the top of a steep bank was the main London to Bournemouth Railway line; this was to figure a great deal in my life, both during the war years and in the later days of my idyllic youth growing up in this wonderful community.

Downstairs there were two rooms and a kitchen, though we knew these by different names. The front room was Mrs Spender's living room and this, like her bedroom, was strictly out of bounds to my family. Even in later years when this room was part of our home, we as young people were still not allowed to enter. It became my mother's special room and was used only for important visitors. The only time it was open to us was once a year at Christmas. During the war years we had the back sitting room that looked out over the garden and the small kitchen next door. However, for reasons I cannot fathom, we knew the sitting room as the kitchen and the kitchen itself as the scullery.

And hanging on a hook behind the back door of this small room was that insignificant looking black bag containing all of our documents. Had the house been destroyed by enemy bombing and we didn't have it, not only would we have been homeless, but we would have lost the ability to identify ourselves and to get the meagre amounts of food and clothing which were only available when accompanied by coupons from the ration books.

Each time the siren wailed my mother reacted the same way, 'Grab the black bag and get straight to the shelter,' she shouted to either Sue or Pat, whoever was closest. I was lying in my drawer while Mrs Spender wrapped my two sisters and my brother George in pullovers and coats and got them out of the house. As young as I was I still felt a panic, an overwhelming feeling of being overlooked. I was convinced they had forgotten all about me.

This was far from the truth, of course. I was such a young child and still being breast fed so needed more things prepared. When this was done, the drawer was pulled out of the sideboard and carried, with me inside it, out to the shelter. In early 1941 this was the cellar of the Brook Inn, a charming public house situated on the corner of Belgrave Road at its junction with busy Portswood Road. Here we would wait through the night in comparative silence. This was undoubtedly brought on by fear. The children would sit as close to their mothers as possible while the bombs rained down around us, impacting not with a bang but a crump which shook the ground. This must have been so unnerving to people who knew what was happening and were not cushioned by youth and innocence as I was. They lived in perpetual fear, knowing that the next bomb that came whistling out of the sky could so easily fall on them.

When the all clear did eventually sound the landlord of the Brook Inn, Mr Jewit, told everyone to stay where they were until he had gone outside to see if Belgrave Road was still standing. Each time, to everyone's enormous relief, he returned to announce that no hits had been suffered, so we could all return safely home. Belgrave Road came through the war relatively unscathed. All around us, in so many parts of Southampton, houses and businesses were being destroyed. But, even though railway lines were a prime target for the German bombers, we suffered not a single loss. I know of only one bomb that actually fell in Belgrave Road. It was an incendiary and landed in a place that had no buildings. One of the residents, Mr Aldridge, raced down to the spot and defused the device, rendering it harmless. This was a very brave thing to do and earned that piece of ground the nickname of 'The Bombed Buildings'. That is how we described the place that became our playground, where we played endless games.

Later in 1941 large red-brick shelters were erected, the nearest of these being right outside our house. Of these shelters I can remember nothing, but my sister Pat has since told me there were rows of bunks along each wall, the rest of the shelter being very bare and basic. No-one got around to sleeping in the bunks though. How could you sleep when the German air force, in a campaign of sheer ferocious hatred, were doing their best to completely destroy the town and everyone in it? A task of which I am proud to say they failed.

Of my father I knew absolutely nothing at the time. I didn't even know I was supposed to have one. He was away fighting the might of the German army and there was every reason to suppose he might never return, as so many didn't from that bitter war. So to cushion us from this possibility, Victorian stoicism once more came into force and children were told nothing. After all, you can't mourn for someone you know nothing about. Early every morning, while the family was still asleep, my mother, in company with one of the neighbours, ran up to the police station in the adjacent Portswood Road. Although exhausted from yet another freezing and terrifying night in the air raid shelter, they needed to look at the bulletin board outside. This listed all the fallen and wounded military personnel from Southampton. Fortunately my father's name was never there. However, as children we were kept completely in the dark about the man who had been responsible for our entry into the world.

I now know, from a piece written about him in the *Southampton Daily Echo*, from 1944, that he was in Six Commando. Corporal William Marsh, as the *Echo* piece tells us, was a cook. But I have since learned he was much more besides. After joining he came out top in his unit and was selected for commando training. This took place in Scotland, and it was here, along with his fellow recruits, that he was taught the commando way of fighting: scaling cliffs in the dark to attack enemy held positions, and the art of hand to hand combat. This is one of the hardest things to do because it brought men into personal contact with the enemy. The killing was not done with guns or grenades, but from close range. He had to creep up on enemy sentries, grasp them from behind and kill by strangulation, or thrusting a commando knife into their vital organs.

How many of us now, if called upon to do this sort of thing, could actually go through with it? My father, along with many others, did because it was simply their job. He served with Field Marshall Montgomery's forces where he became Monty's personal cook.

During this time he became a dispatch rider. This meant riding a motorcycle at high speed, often passing through enemy-held territory to deliver important documents to the British High Command. This was very dangerous because these riders were a prime target to the enemy and many of them did not survive the war. Corporal Marsh never received a wound during his army service. Even when taking on the equally dangerous job of a sniper, which involved hiding in trees and picking off enemy troops. He has subsequently been described to me as a very brave man, and as his son I am extremely proud of him for that.

One story I have of him from this time came to me recently, and was told by my sister Sue. She was the oldest child and actually knew dad before the war. This was the only time in the whole of his army service that he was home on leave. If I did meet him then, I cannot remember because I would have been too young.

It was following America's entry into the war, prompted by the Japanese attack on their naval base at Pearl Harbour, and just one day after my first birthday on 7 December 1941. Many American soldiers were in this country mingling with the British population and trying out our public houses. They had to get used to warm beer and British licensing hours, as well as the shortages we had to contend with on a daily basis. Because dad was home he spent his evenings in the Brook Inn, and on one of these occasions my mother joined him, leaving us children in the care of Mrs Spender.

There were some GIs in the bar, and once my mother was seated her striking good looks attracted the attention of one of these. He strolled over and placed his hand on the back of her chair in a friendly fashion because he obviously wanted to get to know her. Seeing this, my father drew the Luger pistol he always wore throughout his wartime service. He then calmly placed the barrel of the gun against the GIs temple and said, 'Would you mind taking your hand off the back of my wife's chair?' It isn't surprising the man did as he was asked and left the pub without looking back.

One of my most vivid memories was the dreaded gas mask. The Germans had used gas to attack our troops in the First World War and it was feared they would try the same horrible tactic again. So we were all supplied with the means to survive if this did happen. Although they were designed to save our lives, to us children they were quite simply tortures from hell. The first time my mother put me in a baby version, called a Mickey Mouse because the baby was placed right inside it. The experience was every bit as bad as the larger versions. I screamed the place down, I fought and kicked and did everything I could to get out of the awful thing.

The adult versions were just as bad; dreadful things that went right over the head covering the nose and mouth, with a clear viewing window to look through. They also had a large expenditure hanging down the front that resembled an elephant's trunk, giving the grown-ups a very frightening appearance. I don't think anyone who put one of these things on, or were strapped inside, will ever forget that terrible suffocating feeling, or the horrible sickening smell of rubber.

German U-boats were causing havoc among the ships that provided this country with essential supplies. We had to put up with food supplements like powdered egg and milk. They were awful, but kept us alive and helped us through the war. Despite these hardships, what does stand out in my mind was the way everyone pulled together. This was a united front and it got everyone through these terrible times. Even as children we knew and understood this.

Mr Wilkins, one of the elderly men in the road, told me of a time when, just after an air raid, he carried me out of the shelter. As the roar was heard overhead I excitedly pointed up at the 'lovely aeroplane'. Everyone else was horrified. The aircraft in question was a German bomber and its doors were open. Fortunately for us they had already dropped their bomb load and were simply passing overhead on their way back to base.

Other members of my family that lived outside our road were not so fortunate, namely two of my mother's sisters, Ada and Vickie. In Aunt Ada's case it was early in the war when an incendiary hit her bedroom and set it alight. Fortunately this was spotted as soon as the all clear was sounded and the fire was put out before too much damage had been caused. What happened to Aunt Vickie however was much more serious. She had just married the young man she had met on 6 December 1939, exactly one year before my entry into the world. His name was Lesley, Uncle Les to us of course, and in those early days he and his new bride were living with his parents.

Les was not called up to serve in the armed forces because he was involved in vital work in the Spitfire factory in Southampton. The Germans bombed that factory to ruins but they relocated elsewhere. Production of the super aircraft, that did so much to win the war, managed to go on despite all of the German's frantic efforts to stop it.

On 28 February 1940, he was at home when the siren sounded to announce yet another raid. As he made his way to the Anderson Shelter situated at the bottom of the garden he felt a powerful blast of wind from behind. Conscious of the fact that his feet were no longer in contact with the ground, he was quite literally sent flying through the air and landed at the bottom of the garden, squashed up against the back fence. When he struggled to his feet and looked back there was nothing but a pile of rubble. The house had suffered a direct hit and his family was inside it. I have since spoken to my Aunt Vickie to find out what exactly happened that awful day. This is her version of those events:

> We were all in the house when the siren sounded so Les started out to go to the shelter. We were left inside, meaning to follow him at once. Besides me, there was his mother, father and sister. Just before we started my father-in-law said, 'Bomb, quick, lie on the floor.' I did as he told me, though I heard nothing myself. The next moment there was a terrific noise as a bomb hit the front of the house and demolished it completely. We were all in the kitchen and this collapsed in on top of us, burying us beneath tons of rubble.
>
> My father-in-law was killed outright, but miraculously the rest of us were still alive. I had been by the side of my mother-in-law's large Welsh dresser and this had broken and fallen in on top of me. It trapped my left arm beneath and this, somehow, was the only physical injury I suffered that day. But the wait to dig us out took five hours to complete. I have never forgotten this and I never will. It is the dark I remember so clearly, even more than the choking dust. It shut us into another world and we had no idea at all what was happening outside.
>
> We knew very early on the rescuers were working to free us. They had come as soon as the all clear sounded and shouted, 'Anyone alive down there?' We shouted back as loud as we could, 'Yes we're here.' We didn't realise the work of freeing people trapped under rubble is a slow and painful business. It has to be done with the utmost care to prevent the whole structure from collapsing even further and crushing the victims beneath. The first contact they made after that interminable wait was the body of my father-in-law.

As his body was brought out my husband clearly heard the volunteer workers say, 'This one is for the morgue.' It must have been awful for him as he couldn't see which one of us it was. He just knew that at least one was dead; had he lost his wife or not? It was just as bad for me as I didn't know if Les was alive. We finally met up at the hospital where we were all taken after the rescue. This brought about a bond between us that lasted through all the years of our marriage, made stronger by the day we nearly lost one another. The bomb hit the house on the evening of 28 February, so we have always said I was buried in February and rescued in March.

It was not Hitler or his hated air force who so nearly claimed my young life, but that ever-present danger of the accident in the home. This was in late 1942. I had then, and still have today, the desire to do everything at breakneck speed. I was the same with learning to walk. Apparently I was not interested in crawling around. As soon as it could be managed I was up on my feet and blundering about.

On the day of the accident my mother had just made a pot of tea. I was, as usual, tottering around on my little legs and constantly falling over. Sensing something near, I instinctively reached out for support to break my fall; this turned out to be the table cloth. As I fell I dragged this with me, bringing the large enamel tea pot with it and tipping its scalding contents all over me. It is of course just as well I have no actual memory of that terrible event.

Mrs Spender had some nursing experience and she sent my mother out to get the services of one of the neighbours. Eddy Biggs lived a few doors away and drove a taxi. She was to get him at all costs and without delay. What Mrs Spender did next saved my life, as my mother was told by hospital staff later. She snatched me up and with a pair of very sharp scissors cut all of my clothing off. Unfortunately much of my skin came with it. She then wrapped me up in anything she could find, putting nothing at all on the burns, and this was vitally important as well. Meanwhile, my mother had burst into the home of Eddy Biggs and dragged him away from his dinner. Then, along with Mrs Spender, all three of us were thrust into the back of Eddy's taxi and the mercy dash to the hospital began.

I now know from what I have been told over the years that my condition was very serious. My whole body had swollen up during the trip to the hospital and for some time no one was allowed to see me. It would have been too upsetting for anyone to have seen the pitying state I was in. I was given little chance of survival because pneumonia, brought on by shock, had set in. However, if I have one thing in life it is the will to survive. This has been inherited from my family. Somehow, after more than six weeks in hospital I made it through.

I still carry the scars of that awful accident both physically and mentally. My upper arms are scarred where I lost so much skin that day. Even now when I see films warning of dangers in the home, showing children reaching up towards handles of saucepans boiling on the kitchen stove, I go cold all over and have to look away.

In my subconscious, I relive that day in 1942 when it happened to me. It is a constant reminder of the time when I was required to cheat death.

My mother's first reaction after returning from the hospital was to throw the enamel teapot as far away as she could. It joined a lot of other unwanted Belgrave Road rubbish over the fence on the railway land beyond. She had been told by the doctors that this contributed to the awful plight of her son. Enamel holds the heat and, while this is fine for making tea, it did me a lot more harm. So much had been taken out of me, in that momentous fight for life, that I had a lot of nervous reactions as a child; and we all know that other children are not very sympathetic. Many taunts came my way, and these often led to fights.

It makes me wonder how my mother coped with having a young family during the Blitz. Food and clothing shortages, and now her youngest son not expected to live. How tough did people have to be then? The answer was very hard and very determined. She did cope, we did survive, and we saw out 1942. Southampton may have been very badly mauled but we were still here and carrying on as best we could. One other memorable character joined our family that year when we acquired a kitten. It was a female – ginger and white – and because she arrived in the middle of the Blitz, my mother called her that. Blitz, or Blitzie, as she was affectionately known. Blitzie was with us throughout my childhood and teenage years and died eventually at the grand old age of twenty-one. In those years she became another member of the family and shared the highs and lows of life along with the rest of us; she was a much-loved family pet.

As I grew older I became more aware of things around me. I can recall, for instance, my brother George and me looking through the tiny chinks in the blackout curtains towards the end of the war. Searchlights still probed the night skies whenever there was any threat of enemy aircraft overhead. We were thrilled to see those huge beams shining up at the night skies. The railway was very prominent too. One time, after a particularly bad raid on Southampton airport, a train was carrying the wounded slowly into the heart of town so the victims could be taken to hospital. Anxious relatives climbed over the railway fence and ran alongside the train, trying to find out if their loved ones were among the dead or injured.

On a much happier note, there was a signal just beyond our back garden, and American troop trains would often stop at this. The GIs, knowing how short we were of essential foodstuffs, would throw all sorts of goodies from the windows, from sweets and chocolate to precious tinned food. This was always the signal to scramble. No matter what you had been doing it was grab a bag and get over the railway fence. Anything you picked up went into the bag to be carried home in triumph, except for the American soldiers who fell out of the train and landed on the bank among us. We put them back.

Even here the community spirit prevailed. Living on the railway side of the road we, along with all our neighbours, had an unfair advantage over the families opposite. They were just as short of food so whatever was gathered up was put together and shared out to all the residents of Belgrave Road. This was our main survival weapon: neighbour helped neighbour and even the kids shared what we had.

There was one exception to this though. From 1943 onwards things started to get better for us, as more and more German aircraft were shot from the skies. It became fashionable for the older children to look for and collect shrapnel. My two sisters were especially active here. This was to be found in the streets and even on the roofs of the air-raid shelters. When found this became private property. Many children boasted large collections of these mementos of the carnage going on around us. It was a symbol of our side's triumph over our enemies.

Another favourite pastime, conducted away from parental vision, was to go up to any American soldiers walking the streets of our town. Lots of them were here in late 1943 and early 1944 in preparation for the great invasion of Europe on D-Day. When presented with this chance we all said the same thing, 'Got any gum chum?' The answer was always yes. We were rewarded with chewing gum, which the Americans had in endless supplies. If we were lucky we also got chocolate. Our parents were not aware we did this and certainly would not have approved. America might have been on our side, but we were not allowed to speak to strangers, and definitely never to ask for anything from anyone.

Sue and Pat would have been in trouble if my mother ever found out they were responsible for her being confronted by two GIs on her doorstep. Little did she know that her two daughters had used the gum chum ploy but had been asked, 'Where do you two live?' I'm sure these men, who were so far from home, only wanted to be friendly. Unfortunately my mother, who had been through a very strict Victorian upbringing, didn't see it like that. She was horrified that two complete strangers wanted to come into her home to speak to her. She was having none of it and slammed the door in their faces. She then rushed through the house to firmly shut and bolt the back door as well. What those two Americans thought I can only now wonder. But I can hazard a guess they thought the British people, who they were over here to help, were somewhat peculiar.

What we children didn't know was the scale of the build-up to D-Day. We knew Southampton was teeming with troops from other countries; America, Canada, France and Holland. This was evident all the time as we went about our daily lives. But at the docks every sort of craft was moored and ready to go as soon as the orders were given. Assault craft, landing craft, tank carriers and many more were there in preparation for the biggest ever seaborne assault on enemy-held territory. On 6 June 1944 this great invasion took place, taking our chewing gum suppliers with it. Our parents, of course, were greatly excited by this, because once the allied forces set foot in German-occupied Europe and began the job of driving them out, the end of the war would not be far away.

For us at home it was not now so vicious, although Hitler had started using the dreaded V1 flying bombs, known here as doodlebugs. These made such a noise when in flight, but when the fuel ran out and the engine died it was the signal to dive for cover. In the silence that followed, only the rush of air as the bomb fell could be heard, before the sound of the explosion as it landed. Our only defence against this bomb was if our defenders managed to shoot them down when in flight. Fortunately our boys were doing very well in Europe, and when at last, on the 8 May 1945, it was suddenly all over we couldn't believe what was happening.

The announcement of the end of the Second World War came during the day while Sue, Pat and George were not at home. They were at a place called Portswood Secondary Modern, leaving each morning and returning home in the afternoon. On that day however they came in early, having been sent home because of the wondrous news of the end of hostilities in Europe. They came bounding into the house, caught up in an excitement they didn't really understand.

This same feeling was already manifested in Belgrave Road. All the adults, who were usually so sensible, were outside hugging and kissing each other; while the cry repeated from so many throats rang out, 'It's over, the wars over!' When all the children were assembled a marvellous thing happened. Up until now there were two things everyone, not just the children, had to be careful about: making a noise and, even more important, showing a light. Both would have helped our German enemies to pinpoint their targets and do even more harm than they actually did. Now, with nothing more to fear in this direction, the hated blackout curtains were being ripped down in all the houses and taken out into the road. Here they were piled in the middle along with any other rubbish that could be found.

Then, to our enormous excitement, all the children were given large pots and pans, tin bowls, and anything else that when hit with a stick would make a very loud noise. We were then set free, and for the first and only time in our lives told to do just that; and how we took advantage. For hours that went on into the night we ran up and down Belgrave Road banging our pans, making an ear-splitting noise. When at last darkness came, the heap of rubbish in the centre of the road was set alight. I will never forget the sight of that bonfire and how it burned so fiercely. It wasn't just a celebration fire; it was a light after so much darkness; a freedom from fear and welcome to a life of peace once more, with the threat from Nazi Germany now finally and irrevocably crushed.

The celebrations lasted well past midnight and when the children, now thoroughly worn out, went to bed, another milestone in my young life was reached. As I lay there, I could see, for the first time ever, out of the bedroom window. The houses opposite stood out in the glare of the still burning bonfire. In place of the blackout curtains, now burning with the rest in the road outside, was clear glass. Looking out at the road I was to grow up in was a wonderful sight that I have never forgotten.

Later on we had the victory street parties. Belgrave Road, along with so many other places in Southampton, rose to the occasion. Sitting at long trestle tables that reached from one end to the other, we had a wonderful time. There were cakes and all sorts of goodies that we had not even tasted before. Our parents had pooled their meagre rations to produce this. There was music and real laughter and oh how I enjoyed it all.

Yes ,the war was over and life could now start getting back to how it should be. There were quite a few more years of food and clothing shortages. Many other things, including sweets, would still be rationed. But we could live with that; after all hadn't we been doing just that for the past six years?

I, along with many other kids born around the same time, was just coming up to five years old. What I didn't know, and was about to find out, was that after all the joviality had subsided we were going to have to face that place my parents casually referred to as 'school'.

# 2

# *Peace at Last*

The end of the Second World War had a great effect on me. Now I was able to leave the house alone. Not only during the day, but as it was late spring, for short periods in the evenings as well. This was hard to believe at first because we had been so closely watched during the war. Such was the horror of the constant bombardment that very young children were never allowed out of their mother's sight. Now I was going to be able to discover, not only the area where I lived, but also boys and girls of my own age. We were ignorant of so much that normal streetwise children would know. All we had experienced up until now were bombs, shrapnel, anti-aircraft guns, American soldiers and everything else that goes with a country in the midst of a war.

The older children had gone to school together throughout the hostilities, many times having to rush from their classrooms during air raids. They also played together, but the young ones saw each other only briefly. Most of the time this was from behind our mother's skirts as we all sat waiting in the shelters.

Belgrave Road was riddled with back ways designed to allow the dustmen do their job. Household rubbish, in those days, was put into bins made out of corrugated tin and kept at the bottom of the back garden. On collection day the men came round and transferred the waste into their own bin. These were then heaved onto their shoulders and carried to the lorry parked in the road. Vegetable peelings were also collected on a weekly basis to be used as pigs swill. Nothing in those barren days was ever wasted.

They of course were one of the first things we discovered. Tailor-made for games that required a lot of chasing and hiding, we were to do a great deal of both over the next ten years or more. Before my generation raced around these back ways, the former residents of Belgrave Road used these same cut ways to avoid capture by the police. I can believe that because to know your way around these was a very definite advantage and a great way to lose anyone you didn't want to see.

Another frequent use was as a shortcut to the main Portswood Road. The nearest entrance was right opposite my home, a partly covered narrow cut way that broadened out at the halfway point as it reached the limits of the back gardens on that side. It then widened considerably and veered first right then left, leading up to the main road. There were houses on both sides, and at the top were the shops. Spagagna's shoe repair to the left and Sangster's barbers on the right. Both of these were still trading twenty years later when I finally left home. From here, going in either direction were the shops that were such a part of our lives. An area that stretched from Woodmill Laundry in Swaythling, to our right, to a shopping complex called Portswood Junction to our left.

During this time everything a family needed was very strictly rationed. The war had drained this country's resources to such an extent that everything was in short supply. Each family in Great Britain was only allocated so much of essential items such as food and clothing. It didn't matter how much money you might have, not that we had very much, but if you didn't have those all important ration coupons then you would not be served. In these days, long before supermarkets, you needed to visit several shops and where there was more than one of the same type of shop in the area it was necessary to be registered with one of them.

Our meat, like most of the other residents of Belgrave Road, came from Martin's so this was the butcher shop we always went to when our mother bought our weekly ration. If we went to the other shop, they would look up and see we weren't registered there and we wouldn't be able to buy any, even if we had the money and ration coupons. Howard's was very much a smaller business than Martin's in Swaythling, but they did have a good clientele from the roads on the opposite side to them. I never really knew much about this shop although I passed it on a daily basis.

Lock's sold the best fish and chips in the whole of Southampton, while Whitlock's was a sweets and tobacco shop. Often in later years, while waiting to attend Sunday school at a little hall directly opposite, we would gaze up Sirdar Road until we saw the man himself making his way down to open up. Leaving his house he would look down to his shop to see a crowd eagerly looking back waiting for him to arrive. Then we would follow him inside to spend our few pennies on sweets to take to Sunday school with us.

Another small shop was run by two very nice ladies; this was Bailey's. There was always time to talk and browse, and Mrs Bailey was never too busy to attend to her little customers. We needed help, because it wasn't just the price of sweets that was important to us. A far more serious consideration was how many priceless coupons each transaction required. Once these were gone there would be no more sweets until the next allocation of ration books, so we were exceedingly careful in our use of these. Mrs Bailey always advised on the sweets that had the lowest coupon requirements; this was a huge help to us and we loved and appreciated her so much because of it.

There was a small shop selling writing paper, ink and blotting paper, but their main trade came from lending books for a small fee. My mother was a regular customer here and rented her favourite reading material from this shop. These were always books about romance or, slush, as we called it. One of our favourite places was the smithy. What great fun we had here watching the elderly blacksmith in his torn leather apron, as he placed the red-hot shoes onto the horse's hooves. Skilfully shaping these before they were fitted, he never seemed to mind us crowding into his doorway to watch.

Next to the smithy was the newspaper shop where most of our parents bought their daily papers. Beyond this the Catholic church stood at the other end of Belgrave Road. This was a green tin building and not one that any of us ever entered having been brought up as Church of England. But we all knew this place because it was a boundary over which we were not allowed to pass unless suitably accompanied; this was our area of Southampton. I have mentioned Woodmill Laundry, and this formed the boundary down the other end of Swaythling. This was also not to be passed without escort.

One of the cottages was steeped in myth and rumour because of the elderly lady who lived there. None of us, not even our parents, knew anything about her because she kept very much to herself. We didn't even know this lady's name. So we made up our own scary stories about her. These were taken so seriously that this particular cottage was given a very wide berth indeed.

It was, of course, the home of a horrible witch, complete with black cat, who would use her spells to turn children into ghastly little creatures if she ever got her hands on us. We could easily reach the back of this property because the cut ways ran past, but there was a very high wall. Inevitably, in later years, we became braver and far more daring, so challenges were made to climb over and sneak into her garden. I never rose to these because I had a very healthy fear of witches and wanted nothing to do with this one. I wonder now, so many years, later what that elderly lady was really like. For all we knew she could have been a very nice person indeed.

Near to and in sight of the laundry was a road I came to know very well for two reasons. This was Mayfield Road where my grandparents lived. My mother was part of a family of eight girls and two boys. But not all of her childhood was spent here. Although large families were commonplace, this didn't make it any easier to cope. Feeding and clothing that many children was a daunting task. So she was farmed out and raised mostly by her grandmother. This is how she met my father; they knew one another as children because he lived beyond Portswood Junction in Dukes Road, which was the next street.

Because she had so many relatives we were taken around to see them quite often. This was exciting because we travelled on a tram. There were two types, open top and closed in, and both were a wonder to me. I would hold tightly onto my mother's hand and run along beside her. My little legs went like pistons trying to keep up as we went along the cut leading to the tram stop outside Lock's fish and chip shop. Here we would wait until it rattled along on the rails in the middle of the road, powered by overhead cables.

We had to walk out into the centre of the road to board. I ran up the stairs every time then sat on the hard wooden seats, from where I could see so much of the shattered city of Southampton. The drivers stood with handles in front of them which they seemed to turn a lot. I never really discovered what these did because the days of the trams were numbered and they were shortly to be replaced by buses. Most of those early trips were either to my mother's elder sister, Aunt Ada, or to the top of Bevois Valley, a bit further on, to great-grandmother's house.

This was something George and I never enjoyed. Great-grandmother lived with her sister, our Great-aunt, who was extremely house proud. She glared at us with deep suspicion, daring us to make any noise or mess. We did neither, both of us were fully aware taht it was not a good idea to upset a lady like this. She was the sort of woman who went out and cleaned the windows every time it stopped raining outside, just in case anything nasty had come down with the rain water. So we sat rigidly still and quiet, until mum mercifully said it was time to go home. That time could never come fast enough.

From those tram rides I got to know what the town of my birth was like, especially the bomb sights along the route; and there were many of these. Southampton had taken a severe pounding from the Luftwaffe and everywhere you looked there were large areas of ruins where not a single building was left untouched. We were to find and play in so many of them before Southampton was rebuilt. At Portswood Junction we passed the police station, an imposing building where my mother had gone so many times to check the bulletin boards. Next to this was the tram depot. Both of these were very drab Victorian buildings, to be avoided as far as we were concerned.

All of these things were waiting to be discovered, but as 1945 progressed the important thing for me was getting to know my new friends. Like everything else in Belgrave Road friendships were easily made and kept up. But as I shyly came out into the road for the first time on my own, in late May, I looked with wonder at several children my own age, who were doing the same thing. Not everyone was here. Some had been evacuated for the duration of the war to safer and quieter locations, and had not yet returned to their roots in Southampton.

Some instant and very long-lasting friendships began at this time. Although we had all been together for the VE-Day celebrations, these were crowded and noisy times with both adults and children present. Now we were meeting on our own ground for the first time, in a world free of war and the threat of death from the skies.

I met the stalwarts of the road. Boys such as David Simmonds, whose gran lived right at the top in No.121, next to the Brook Inn car park. Dave didn't actually live here; he and his sister Glenda lived with their parents in a place called South Stoneham. They were both born at their grandparent's house though, and so were legitimate Belgrave Road children. They certainly spent most of their youth with us and we were delighted with them both. Victor Warrender was the youngest member of his family and the same age as me. There was also Bobby Westmore, who came from a very large family, but played with us as he was in our age group. I still don't know exactly how many brothers and sisters Bobby had but there were quite a few. Large families were quite normal in those days.

On the opposite side was the house occupied by the Whelan family, who were a great influence on my life as I grew up. Not only was Edwin, the eldest of the family, a great personal friend of mine in later years, but I also got on very well with his sister, Sylvia, and younger brother, Ken. Mr and Mrs Whelan were very different from so many adults. In most cases the main rule, as far as youngsters were concerned, was that children should be seen but not heard. Very few of them had any real time for us. In consequence our opinions were never asked for and wouldn't have been listened to if we had dared try and make them. Edwin's parents, however, actually talked to us, especially his father. I can remember endless sessions with this likeable man as he told us stories and took time to explain things.

It took a little longer to get to know Edwin because he was away on at least two occasions at the Lord Mayor Treloar Orthopaedic Hospital in Alton, Hampshire. This was another world away as far as we were concerned. Born with his fingers joined together, he would have gone through life with webbed hands without these operations. They were a complete success and Edwin's hands became quite normal afterwards. These were carried out by a noted surgeon named Sir Archibald McIndoe. During the war he did valuable work on the faces and bodies of our brave Spitfire pilots who had been badly burned during aerial battles with the Germans. When we found this out, Edwin became quite a hero himself.

Directly across the road from us were the Priestly family, two girls and three boys. Brian was a month or two younger than me and his brother, Peter, was a year younger. Both of these joined our gang. Going down the road we had Phillip Scoulart, Keith Masterman and Timmy Donaldson, whose father was of ethnic origin. This made no difference to any of us at all. There was no race discrimination and Timmy was a much liked and welcome member of our group. His father was given the same respect we had been taught to give all grown-ups.

Further down was the very popular Trevor Johnson. He was two or three years older but often joined us. Trevor was a natural leader and every one of us recognised that. We followed wherever he led without the slightest hesitation. Next to the bombed buildings was another boy, John Bates, who became a great friend. He was an only child, but he made up for this by spending his time with us.

I must not leave out the Belgrave Road rebel. His name was Pat Marriott. Six months younger than me, he was a mixture of scallywag, daredevil and tearaway. He had three brothers and two sisters, most of them were older than us, with the exception of Dave, who was the same age as my brother George. We treated him with caution because he was unpredictable, to put it mildly. Every game, every dare that had an element of risk, and all of the completely mad and dangerous things we got up to over the next few years originated from Pat. Nothing ever phased him, he was quite literally game for anything, which meant we had to be as well.

So there we were, a bunch of ragamuffins wearing hand-me-down clothes that the older children had grown out of. We approached each other with caution but, after staring for a while, a curious thing happened – we just started to play together. First a chasing game up and down the road then we hid behind the shelters. We quickly found out that when, such a short time ago we were encouraged to make noise, this had been for a very special reason. Now, for the first time, and for many times after that, we were shouted at by various adults, 'Keep the noise down, go and play at your own end you kids.'

As the year came to its end, some of the girls came back from evacuation. What strange creatures they seemed to us at first – Pauline Ayres, Doreen and Maureen Pickard, two sisters who lived just a few doors away, Dianne Cope and Vickie Masterman who was no relation to Keith's family, and several others I can't even now remember.

There was also the Selby family. Andrew was the same age as me and so quickly became not just a close friend but a member of the Belgrave Road gang. His sister Diana was three years older. Appearing grown-up to us, in those early years I knew very little about her. As we grew older however her behaviour became noticeable. Not just to us, but to our parents as well. She was a rebel, and, along with her school friend Sally Farlow, who lived close by in Broadlands Road, this quickly became a talking point. Life was still ruled by Victorian morals at the time, and children had to conform, or face the consequences. Diana Selby would have none of that and did things her own way, which meant we had to learn to avoid her.

She always gave us boys a very hard time indeed if we gave her the chance. We never called for Andrew at home because of the taunts and sneers we got from Diana. If no-one was looking she would hit out at us with her fists, feet or anything she happened to have at the time. We thought she was mad, but over a period of time the reasons for her erratic behaviour, which began in 1946, became very clear.

The story of Diana Selby began in 1939, a year before I was even born. She was evacuated and sent to a farm in Kent. This was owned and run by a couple who had two children of their own. Diana knew them as Aunty Daisy and Uncle Paul. She was given her own little room on the top floor of the large farmhouse and soon got over the shock of being away from her home in Southampton. There was always plenty to eat and so much space to play in during the day.

It was the nights however that soon began to fill this little girl with terror. Uncle Paul started to come up to her room after dark, when everyone else was asleep, to make sure she was tucked up properly. At four years old she never understood the strange feelings her body was subjected to while her uncle altered the bedclothes. Then he would whisper to her that she must not tell anyone about this. Gripping her little wrist in his big farmer's hand until she cried out with pain, he would hiss at her, 'It will be our little secret, wont it?'

This horror began happening on a regular basis, and poor little Diana would lie awake, dreading the footsteps on the stairs and the stealthy opening of her bedroom door. This man regularly assaulted her so when her mother, at the beginning of 1941, decided she wanted both her children home with her whatever the consequences, it was such a blessed relief. The episode so affected Diana Selby that she convinced herself that all men, as well as boys, were as bad as this awful child molester in Kent. She soon started her own war on the male sex.

Understandable as this may be now, none of us knew about it at the time, and wouldn't have understood it if we had. We knew nothing about sex and certainly wouldn't have suspected that an adult person could do something like that to a child. Adults were trusted people and although they frequently shouted at us, and smacked us when we did wrong, they wouldn't ever really hurt us would they? Sadly the answer to that is the same as it is today. Child molesters were plying their evil trade then as well. They just weren't discovered, or if they were their despicable crimes were always swiftly covered up. Diana Selby and Sally Farlow loomed in and out of our lives as we grew up, and became two of the very few people we kept clear of whenever possible.

It was late summer, 1945, when my mother took me up the cut to the tram stop to start the longest journey I had made so far. Moving past Portswood Junction along the top of Bevois Valley, we turned right into a road I hadn't been down before, which led to the Stag Gates at London Road. A long time ago these gates did have big models of stags on each post but no-one even remembered them being there. We got off and went along to a very large hall filled with rows and rows of second-hand clothing. After checking to see if my mother had the required coupons the assistant asked what she wanted. She told him she needed clothes for her young son who was about to start school.

Although not new, these clothes were in good condition, so I gained my first suit for special wear. At last, not one that had been handed down to me by my brother George, or one of the older boys in the road; this made me feel very proud. Admittedly this suit had once been owned by someone else, but getting it from here we didn't know who that was. With all our other clothes we certainly did know who the previous owners had been.

There would be a knock at the door and one of the Belgrave Road neighbours would be holding up some clothes, 'My son has grown out of these Mrs Marsh,

but there's plenty of wear in them yet. I'm sure they'll fit your little Jimmy a treat.'
I would then be sent upstairs to try them on. My next clothes for playing or for
Sunday wear were then gratefully received. Looking back on it now I didn't mind
second-hand shirts, shoes or even socks. But it was a stigma to have to wear trousers
that once belonged to an older boy, to go around in fact wearing someone else's
trousers.

The suit consisted of a grey jacket with matching grey short trousers reaching
to just above knee level, a grey shirt, and a coloured pullover. These were worn
with black shoes and knee-length socks. Just a few days later, I was wearing these
when my mother took me up the cut again and out into Portswood Road, past the
Newlands Hotel to the next turning on the right. Following this down we crossed
a bombed out section and arrived in Somerset Road. There stood a large building
looking somewhat grim in the morning light. Holding tight to my mother's hand I
went through the gates, up a slope turning sharply to the left, then up another slope
to finally enter the building through a side door.

We passed a cloakroom that had wash basins all along one wall, before coming
out into the place they called the hall. This was rapidly filling with mothers and
children, among whom were the rest of the Belgrave intake. As we stood there in
this strange place we were introduced to a large lady called Mrs Andrews. Stooping
down to give me a kiss on the cheek my mother started to walk away towards the
exit door.

Every time I had been out during the whole of my life so far it had been with
my mother, except on the few recent occasions when I had been allowed to play
with my new friends. Even then the rules had been strict – never speak to strangers
and never go off on your own. Now she was walking away and leaving me behind.
This wasn't right. If mummy is leaving then I have to go as well. So I tried to follow,
only to find the restraining hand of Mrs Andrews on my shoulder, 'No dear you are
to stay here, you will see mummy again later on.'

It took a few seconds for this to sink in. Screaming panic then took over. I had
been abandoned in this horrible place and was having none of it. I kicked and
screamed and fought to get away and run after my mother, joined by most of the
other kids there. Mrs Andrews though had been through this many times before.
Generations of children had been just as panicky as we were on their first encoun-
ter with this school. Presented with a class of near hysterical children she knew
exactly what to do. She had to give us a reason to want to stay, and she had a secret
weapon.

After a big struggle, she got us into the baby classroom to the right of the main
hall. Sitting at the little desks still sobbing our hearts out, she produced from her
desk bowls of jam tart and custard. Now this got our attention very quickly; we
didn't have things like this at home. We hadn't even seen custard before and it
looked like a dream. When we started to eat it we were all of the same opinion.

Even though the custard had been made with one of the dreadful curses of those hard times, powdered milk, the end result was wonderful. I can confirm, with great authority, the truth of the saying that the way to a man's heart is through his stomach, because it works just as well with five-year-old little boys. Mrs Andrews had a long-standing arrangement with the school dining room, who kept her supplied with these treats to aid her in her conquest of generations of upset boys and girls. This then was my introduction to Portswood Infants.

Opened in 1905 as a bright new school, it was meant to be large and adequate for staff and pupils, and an end to children being taught in overcrowded and cramped conditions. All this was probably true back in those days. But now, forty years and two World Wars later, the place looked anything but exciting and certainly far from new. But we were here now and had to learn to cope. Most of us did, with just two exceptions. Edwin Whelan and, for the short time he attended Portswood School before transferring to one nearer his parent's home, David Simmonds.

On that first morning we were let outside for something Mrs Andrews said was playtime. This meant running around on the infant's side of the playground, that lay between our small school – containing infants and juniors up to the age of eleven – and the much larger building on the other side, which was the senior school. To our right the older girls had their playground and we were told we must not, on any occasion, stray across and mix. They needn't have worried. These girls looked enormous to us, just like teachers in fact, and we automatically stayed well clear of them.

We all huddled close together. I was perhaps more fortunate than most, as my brother George, just a year and a half older than me, was in the same part of the school, so I was able to find him. Also, both of my sisters, Sue and Pat, aged eight and ten respectively, were there as well. This was a great comfort to me in this strange and frightening place.

Edwin however had no-one, and as Mrs Andrews had told him he could go he took her quite literally. As far as he was concerned this meant he could go home. For him school didn't seem anywhere near as bad as it did for the rest of us, just an hour in that little classroom. It's a wonder he made it back safely. We had never been to this part of town before and he had been brought here by his mother. So how did he find his way home so accurately, crossing a main road in order to do it? David Simmonds did this on a regular basis too, with no more success than Edwin, each time both were marched back to school.

At lunchtime that day, known to us then as dinnertime, Sue, Pat and George collected me and we came home to eat. Food was still strictly rationed so this was our only substantial cooked meal of the day. It consisted mainly of potatoes that my mother was able to obtain in reasonable supply from Chandler's greengrocery shop. Because the proprietor knew her so well and knew she had four children to feed, a few extra potatoes were added to the rationed amount each week. Not strictly legal but extremely helpful in those hard times.

With these she would sometimes make a stew, providing she could get the meat and vegetables. Or, and this was my personal favourite, egg and chips. To do this, and, share between four children she would break two eggs into the frying pan, mixing the yokes so they fried together in one piece. When done, this whole egg was divided into four quarters and we were given one each with chips.

It was then back to school for the afternoon session – a shock for me as I thought I was home for the rest of the day. But surrounded by my sisters and brother, with mother along as well to ensure I got back into school properly, I had very little choice but to march back to that horrible building. Afternoon school ended at quarter to four for the infants and juniors. George and I were usually out much faster than Sue or Pat, who had to wait until four o'clock before their afternoon ended, so we would wait for them to come out. Then all four of us raced home.

Our tea was always the same from that year onwards, and, for so many after – bread and jam. This meant bread with margarine, since butter was far too expensive and hard to come by, and then topped with plum jam. I emphasise this because it was always plum jam and never any other variety. Bought in 2lb jars, this was cheaper than any other so I grew up not knowing there was any alternative. My mum also had an arrangement with the manager of the local Lowman's bakery shop. She was told that as she had a large family to feed, providing she could get to the shop at six in the morning, she could buy yesterday's left over bread at one penny a loaf. My mother needed no prompting here. Always up by five every morning, it was easy for her to slip on her coat and hurry to this shop. A bargain like this was far too good to miss.

There was another interesting thing about this regular diet of bread and jam. It wasn't just us kids who ate it; Blitz the cat had the same thing. There was no cat food for sale in those days, and we wouldn't have been able to afford it if there had been. As soon as the four of us were seated at the table Blitz would come running into the house. This was mostly through the back door, but sometimes if the back window of the kitchen was open she would scramble up the wall and come in that way. Then she would meow very loudly until her portion of bread and jam, cut up into small manageable pieces, was put down. Every day she pounced on this with relish and, like us, cleared her plate. Cats have always fascinated me with their ability to adapt to any situation. They can be, and very often are, extremely fussy about what they eat. But when food is scarce and there is every chance of them getting nothing at all they, like us, will eat whatever is available. Blitz was living proof of that, though she did get one treat a week – cooked fish – but all through the rest week it was plum jam.

# 3

# Introduction to My Father

As 1945 came to a close and life was settling into a routine, Mrs Spender moved out of the back bedroom and turned the front room into a bedsit. This was to give us more room. Also, back from convoy duty in the Merchant Navy where he was torpedoed on at least one occasion, was a man who became known to us as Uncle Ron. It was his brothers who had been constant visitors to Mrs Spender during the war years when he was away.

Ron Biggs himself was extremely lucky to be alive. His ship had been quite literally blown out from under him by a German U-boat. Very few of our seamen survived an attack by one of these submarines, either dying in the blast from the torpedo, drowning in the bitter cold waters of the North Atlantic, or being machine gunned by the merciless crew responsible for sinking the ship. However, Ron did survive, but only after living through the hell of wondering if the next hail of bullets, which were also being fired from aircraft overhead, would find their mark and tear into his body. The escorting warships were under orders not to pick up survivors, but to go in and try to destroy the hated U-boats. Sometimes however, the captains were compassionate and brave enough to stop and pick our men up, leaving themselves wide open to attack as they did so. So Ron Biggs did come home and in 1946 married Mrs Spender.

As December approached, something happened that I certainly didn't understand – we were shown how to make paper chains. Brightly coloured strips of paper that stuck together when licked, these were put up on the ceiling to decorate the house for Christmas. Fine, it looked wonderful, but what on earth was Christmas?

During the war this had been a sparse affair, with no extra food or lights and certainly no decorations. Families made what they could of it though, sometimes with amazing results. Despite the horrors around them this great tradition went on, with makeshift presents, in homes all over the country. But I, as a very young child, saw no difference from the usual routine and knew nothing about it. Now though, all of us, including me, get caught up in the excitement.

As this event came closer it was explained to me that someone called Jesus, who was the Son of God, had a birthday on 25 December. This was the same month as me so I did wonder if he was the same age. But I also found this completely mystifying. If Jesus was the Son of God, why was he not called Jesus God? And why was his father just called God? There were a few men in Belgrave Road at that time and we had been taught to give them proper respect, always remembering to address them as 'Mister'. So why was God not being addressed as Mr God? Add to this the fact I still didn't know what a father was. None of this really mattered though. The main thing was that this, Mr God, person had invited us to join the celebrations. So whoever Jesus was, he was alright with me. I even thought of offering him the honour of joining our gang, but the problem is I never actually got to meet him. I put that down to the fact that he probably lived at the other end of Belgrave Road.

I will always remember the 25 December 1945; I was still sharing the front bedroom with my mother, and woke up to feel something at the end of my cot. On investigation this turned out to be a little fluffy bear, some plasticine, a jigsaw puzzle and a reading book. There was also a small bag containing an apple, a whole orange and some chocolate. I gazed in awe at my mother, who smiled back at me. Unable to believe this could all be for me, I was told that a big man called Father Christmas had come down the chimney during the night and left them to celebrate the birth of Jesus. That boy again, and I was beginning to like him more and more. I had never in my short life had so much. A whole apple and orange that I didn't have to share with the rest of my family, not to mention a whole bar of chocolate; this was sheer unbelievable heaven.

I fell in love with the fluffly bear and kept him with me for many years afterwards. The big disappointment was the jigsaw puzzle. This was not new and was definitely pre-war. On the front of the box was a picture of some ducks on a pond. I was told that inside was an even bigger version. Eagerly I emptied the box, but it was broken; there were pieces all over the floor in peculiar shapes. Father Christmas must have dropped it. Through my tears it was Mrs Spender who, with a comforting arm around my shoulder, told me this was how the puzzle was supposed to be. My job was to fit the pieces together. It was of course a baby puzzle and, with my families help, I managed to complete it and wonder over the, now-whole, picture of the ducks.

That day was splendid in so many ways. We had a dinner I could only marvel at, with so much on the plate I was sick afterwards from over eating. Only to recover in time to have a large helping of Christmas pudding that had been made by Auntie Ada. I had never eaten anything like it before and once more over indulged. I was sick again, but it was more than worth it.

One thing puzzled me, not just on that day but for quite some time afterwards. mum told me that Father Christmas, who she described as a big jolly man, had come down the chimney to bring us our presents. The problem here was we only used one fireplace in the whole of our part of the house, and it was a kitchen range. A metal fire and oven that had to be black leaded every so often to keep it looking smart. The fire was next to the oven in a very small space indeed with a metal grill in front and a very narrow chimney. If Father Christmas was so big, how in the world had he got down?

During the following year I found out who God was and about his son, Jesus Christ. This was mainly through Sunday school, held in a little hall in Sirdar Road and attended regularly over the next ten years by all the members of my family. As 1946 began I was at last out of my cot and sleeping in a proper bed in the larger back bedroom I shared with George. This is the one that had been occupied for such a long time by Mrs Spender. From the window I could see not only our back garden, but also the railway line. From fast express trains to slower passenger and freight trains, the daily, and nightly, rail traffic never ceased to fascinate me. We also had a wonderful view of the far side of the line alongside the River Itchen. The banks of that river looked so intriguing with tall trees reaching skywards into the distance.

My last memory of the time I spent in the cot in my mother's room was hearing a terrific commotion coming from downstairs. Two cats were fighting right outside our front door, and, since this was wide open, the noise was unbelievable. From across the road one of our neighbours decided to do something to separate them; their solution was to throw a bucket of cold water over the spitting and clawing animals.

Cats, as most people know, hate water, and the effect of being suddenly drenched was for them to burst apart and race off in a panic. One of them flew across the road and disappeared up one of the back cut ways. The other tore inside our wide open front door, straight up the stairs and into the front bedroom. I can still see it now, a rush of ginger fur that disappeared straight up the chimney of the unused fireplace in the corner of the room. Ron Biggs had to come upstairs and wrap his arm in protective sheets and towels, then reach up and try to grab the cat and bring it down from its perch in the chimney. What a commotion that caused; the cat didn't know that he was trying to help it and just spat and clawed. It was a determined battle that Mr Biggs finally won and the cat, still trembling violently, was brought down to safety. After a lot of fussing it was eventually released and presumably found its way home.

A routine was starting to take shape in our family life and this included bath night, which was traditionally on Friday. The girls would go first and when they were dried and downstairs it was George's and my turn. Sharing the same bath, and incidentally the same water, we were allowed a certain amount of playing time before my mother arrived, armed with a bar of very hard Sunlight washing soap.

This was used for washing everything, our clothes and, to our everlasting regret, us as well. Not only was it hard and rough, it had a peculiar smell.

We were washed all over, no part of our small bodies escaping, and when it was time to have our hair done the misery was complete. I can hear mum saying, 'close your eyes', before vigorously applying this awful soap to the top of our heads. Despite our cries, because believe me it hurt, she used her hands to lather it. This ran down over our faces so if we hadn't heeded the warning, the soap went into our eyes, adding to the pain and discomfort. We came out clean but also rubbed raw. Then it was downstairs for cocoa, which was a luxury item, before going to bed.

At school we were learning how to read and write. I could now read the book I had received at Christmas. Mrs Andrew still produced tempting sweet things from the dining room and we were growing to love her, which was more than I could say about the headmaster Mr Huggins. He was an ex-army officer and ran the school in much the same way.

Boys and girls were strictly separated for anything outside of normal classroom activities. So much so, that there was an invisible brick wall built between us. In the hall at morning assembly the girls were on the left and the boys on the right. The two sides never mingled. Mr Huggins would come and take his place at the front, facing the children, then say, 'Good morning boys and girls.' The answer, all said together, was of course, 'Good morning Mr Huggins.' In the case of the boys, we had to salute with the right hand coming smartly up to the position just above the right eye – army style – longest way up, shortest way down. We did this the entire time we were in the infants and juniors, six years in all.

We used every piece of the ground allocated to us at playtime for chasing games where we ran up and down the slope, stopping only when the gate was reached. There was a small covered area for days when it rained but most of the boys, and this certainly included me, loved to be out in it rather than under cover. What the fascination is in getting wet in the rain I have never understood. I just know I loved it and in later years, along with Edwin Whelan, played endlessly near rivers and streams and always ended up getting soaked through.

Mr Huggins was always lecturing us about the dangers. No doubt, through his army service, he was wet through many times and had to go on fighting while his uniform dried on him. Now he was trying to help us avoid the discomfort, and illness, that this can bring. 'Wet clothes,' he would thunder at us, 'if allowed to dry on your body can cause rheumatism in later life. This is a very painful and untreatable illness that none of you would wish to suffer.'

This was very true. Most of us had grandparents who did indeed suffer from this condition. But what was the use of telling little boys between the ages of five and six? Our mothers would always tell us off but that of course just added to the fun. This was, one thing, we did have the chance to get away with; it wasn't considered really naughty, or deliberate disobedience, so we did it time and time again.

The only time we didn't rush to be in water was when we had to wash, and then we did our best to disappear.

In summer there were six whole weeks when we didn't have to go to school. No-one had the money to go away for holidays but that didn't worry any of us. We had never been outside of our hometown anyway. To spend some wonderful days playing in and around our road, as well as exploring yet more of the area where we lived, was satisfactory to us all.

We found that the cut way, beside Martin's the butcher in Portswood Road, led down to a wide area with a large field and a building that seemed to be filled with the sound of animals. This was a slaughter house, known today as an abattoir. Here we would crowd into the doorway, as we did at the blacksmiths, and watch as large bulls, pigs and sheep were brought in and slaughtered for meat. No sooner had the baying and struggling animals been shot, than their carcasses were hanging up on hooks to be cleaned, prepared and sent to butcher shops in and around Southampton. What ghouls we must have been to get so much excitement from watching animals fighting for their lives against men whose job it was to end them, but we did. The bulls and pigs in particular put up such a battle that we soon began to cheer them on.

The highlight of that summer holiday was the demolition of the air-raid shelters. This happened around the time of the wedding of Mrs Spender to Ron Biggs. Every night, as we went to bed, we had to call through the front-room door and remember to say, 'Goodnight Mr and Mrs Biggs', instead of what we had been saying up until now, which was simply, 'Goodnight Mrs Spender.'

The day the big cranes came to knock down the shelters is one I will never forget. I was overwhelmed, as well as frightened, by these huge machines that had a large metal ball attached to a chain. When swung at speed this collided with the brickwork of the shelters, smashing through them and making a very loud noise indeed. Great plumes of brick dust rose into the air around us. When the cranes had finished, the wrecking teams of workmen closed in and cleared the shattered brickwork. The lorries drove away, taking with them the last remains of the shelters that had been so vital to the civilian population during the war. The demolition was compelling for all of us to watch.

This was wonderful because we now had a clear road in which to play. Free from the obstruction of the shelters and with no traffic to contend with, we took full advantage. One of our favourite games, that was played and enjoyed over a number of years, was 'bad-beef-bad'. This was one of the few times when the girls of the road were welcome. For reasons I can only put down to the strict divide that existed we had an unwritten law. Girls could only join in when we were either chasing or hiding. At all other times, whether it was Cowboys and Indians, pirates or any other games involving sword fighting, homemade wooden guns, or general rough and tumble, girls were very definitely excluded. In bad-beef-bad, however, everyone played in delightful harmony.

The game comprised two teams of mixed boys and girls lining up and facing each other, roughly 3 yards apart. One member, with their backs towards the bombed buildings, went forward to the opposing team who stood with outstretched hands. Slapping each one as they went along the line they would say 'bad tomatoes; bad apples; bad potatoes' and so on, occasionally using the red herring of 'bad-beef-bad'. However, when coming face to face with the boy or girl who had been selected to do the chasing, the challenge was 'bad beef'. This was the signal to turn and run down to a line opposite the lamp post, directly alongside the bombed buildings. The chasing boy or girl had to catch as many of the running team as possible. Those caught dropped out until all their team was eliminated. Then, just like cricket, it was all change and the chasing team was the one now being chased. We loved this game and played it endlessly, being told on many occasions to keep the noise down.

Now that street lighting was allowed, we loved to wait for the man whose job it was to turn these on. He came on a bicycle holding a long pole, at the top of which was a hook. With this he skilfully caught the ring in the centre at the top and gave it a sharp tug. This reversed the switch and turned on the light. This of course was repeated at all the lamp posts in the road until they were brightly lit. He must have really disliked us because we willed him to miss, and had great fun, cheering when he had to ride round in a circle to try again. What little brats we were.

Now far more streetwise about the area, I habitually went out with George and some of the older boys – our mother wanting to be sure I was looked after properly. This arrangement didn't suit either of us, in fact we hated it. I wasn't happy being in the company of boys who were so far ahead of me. The kids I played with in the road were the same age and we all got on so well together. George and his friends were just as unhappy. None of them liked having a young kid trailing around after them. I had developed a very nasty temper, flying into a rage and being difficult to control if I wasn't allowed to do whatever I wanted. In consequence I often got my own way, but this just made me even more conceited. But exploring with them did enable me to discover so much more.

Beyond Woodmill Laundry was a hill leading up to High Road in Swaythling. This had, at the far end, one of the public houses we came to know by name, the Hampton Park Hotel. We automatically followed the grown-ups and learned the names of the pubs in the area. Like them, we used these names when needing directions ourselves, or giving them to other people.

But in our early days of discovery it was the road on the opposite side that was holding our attention. This was Woodmill Lane and George had been told about this by some of his friends from school. Crossing a narrow bridge over the railway line, we could see Swaythling station in the distance on one side, and the back gardens of Belgrave Road on the other, then came to the location that gives this wonderful place its name, Woodmill. This is where the beautiful River Itchen flows down from its source in Winchester.

I don't know how this affected the others but I couldn't believe it and simply stood and stared at this marvellous sight. My brother, seeing my excitement, just grinned back at me. The river meandered away to our left before disappearing from view around a bend. There was a fairly wide path running beside it and we knew it wouldn't be long before all of us would walk along to see where it went.

The one thing that didn't quite inspire us that day, or for any other afterwards for that matter, was the council rubbish tip. I still remember watching the dustcarts as they arrived to empty their load of household refuse, and the sight and sounds of the huge flocks of seagulls swooping down onto the food horde. I can also remember the overpowering stench, but over the next few years we managed to get used to this. In one corner was a ruined boathouse; further on there was a corrugated fence which seemed to split the river into two sections. Beyond this was the saltwater side, the fresh water was allowed to flow through a sluice gate, which frightened me the first time I saw it. I didn't like the way it sucked the water down into its depths, it always seemed so menacing.

This same area today is a marvellous country park and the ruined boathouse is a modern rowing and canoeing club. There is a pleasant walkway through open cricket and football pitches, where you can stroll until reaching the other end by Cobden Bridge. Gone are the rubbish tips and in their place, as well as large green spaces, a minigolf course is there to be enjoyed. But in 1946, the scene was very different.

We were fascinated by the large blocks of concrete placed in a row alongside the path. I now know these were anti-tank positions placed there in case the country was ever invaded by the Germans. It never happened of course and these blocks became a challenge to all of us later on. Once able to return here with my friends, free from having to trail along with my big brother, we jumped from one to the other at speed, the object being not to fall off. It didn't pay to do that because, as well as scraped knees and bruised elbows, one boy in particular always thought it was funny and laughed uproariously; this was Pat Marriot.

Pat thought everything was funny, and in fairness he also laughed at himself on the many occasions when accidents happened to him. I always tried not to give him the chance to laugh at me. This was certainly true when we invaded the metal works known as CPC on the corner of Sirdar Road. This was a very dangerous place to be and children should not have been anywhere near it. There was machinery out in the open and unguarded. Edwin Whelan was particularly lucky when he turned on one of these machines. He had a very healthy curiosity about the working of anything he came across. From toys to machines, he always wanted to know how they worked and what they did. This one was a scythe, and when switched on a large steel blade swept down. This was designed to cut through metal and would easily have severed a human limb. Fortunately the noise caused Edwin to jump back and we ran off before any of the workers appeared to shut the machine down, and start looking for the culprits.

We were not allowed in the yard but this had become one of our playgrounds, and we knew our way around better than some of the adult employees. My sister, Pat, had a very nasty accident when she and Sue came across a large concrete pipe. This was big enough for one boy or girl to crawl inside and be pushed along by the others. Pat failed to notice that her hand was outside the rim of the pipe so, when it started to roll, this caused a very painful injury to her fingers.

An old, disused incinerator had an opening where the furnace used to burn. This was just large enough for our small bodies to pass through. Once crowded at the back of this structure we were safe from chasing adults. One of these in particular we targeted; he worked alone in a little workshop and we would appear deliberately within his sight. The result was always the same. Roaring aloud, which prompted us to give him the name of 'grumpy' he came flying out and chased after us. This, of course, was just what we wanted him to do. Pat Marriot would wait longer than the rest of us, running the risk of getting caught. Or even more alarming, leading 'grumpy' to our hideout. It never happened, but Pat played it far too close for comfort, prompting several of the others to copy him.

The big shock that year was our return to Portswood School after the summer holidays. Having moved up a year we were now in the class of the formidable Mrs McGovern. Where Mrs Andrews had been kindness and warmth, Mrs McGovern was strict, unsympathetic, and a firm believer in punishing anything she saw as a misdemeanour – a whack from a ruler was the punishment. During the first few weeks of that autumn term we all felt this across the back of our hands, and boy did it sting. She used it if we so much as talked in class.

Children had to be taught obedience at all times, as well as respect for adults, and punishment was the way this was achieved. Mrs McGovern, and many more like her, were totally ruthless in this department. When that ruler landed she was totally oblivious to our cries. If we were silly enough to do the same thing again she would strike with much more force, on the back of our hands and our legs as well, leaving big red marks. This was our real introduction to life in the 1940s.

Outside of school there were more relatives to be introduced to. The nearest of these was the much loved Grandmother Nicholson. We saw very little of my grandfather as he was away at sea. He was of American origin, coming from the Bowery district of New York, and served all of his sea-going life travelling between this country and America on just two ships. The first of these was the White Star liner *Majestic*, and later, when White Star was taken over by Cunard, the world famous *Queen Mary*. This ship, along with the *Queen Elizabeth*, was already a familiar sight to us. We knew how to tell the difference between them by the number of funnels. The *Queen Mary* had three, while the *Queen Elizabeth*, known affectionately as the *Lizzie*, had two.

We got to know Grandmother Nicholson quickly. She lived at No.25, not very far up Mayfield Road, but it was on the steepest part. We would run up the garden path into the side door that led to her kitchen and through into the living room where she sat by the window. Gran suffered from high blood pressure and was always being prescribed different medicines. As we settled down at her feet she would open the cupboard in her sideboard and show us the latest addition to this collection. The red one for blood pressure, the green one for nose bleeds. Because we loved her, we listened, with a great deal of patience, because this was usually followed by stories of my mother when she was a girl. This was always preceded by the words, 'of course this happened a long time before you were even thought of.'

We had a lot of time for gran, but Granddad Nicholson, when he was at home, tended to frighten us because he was so loud. Eccentric is probably the word that describes him best. In his own way he loved us as much as gran did, it was just he had such a different way of showing it. He would watch as she cut a slice of cake for us, usually Madeira, then shout across, 'There they go again Mother, on the bum.' This, we now know, is an American expression meaning someone is begging. But as we only knew it in the English context, we were always highly embarrassed when he used the word. He was of course only joking, but we never realised this. In fact we didn't understand him at all.

As the year progressed, some products that had not been available since before the war were starting to reappear. I well remember the day Sue, Pat, George and I ran in from afternoon school for our tea to find at the side of each plate a most peculiar-shaped object. It was cylindrical, yellow in colour and bent rather like the bow used in archery. None of us had ever seen anything quite like this before, even Sue, as the oldest didn't know what they were. So after looking at each other for enlightenment, and getting none, we turned to our mother who was standing there smiling at us.

Before any of us had the chance to ask, she told us this funny looking thing was a banana. So now we knew what it was called, but what were we supposed to do with it? Is it food or a toy? For the duration of the Second World War, shipping was acquisitioned for convoy duty and used to transport only the most essential foods as well as weapons. Things like bananas, which were brought here from tropical countries, stopped coming in. 'It's a fruit,' my mother said, 'you can eat it.'

As we dubiously raised it to our mouths to take our first bite, mum realised the mistake we were about to make. 'No, you have to peel it first,' she shouted. Then, taking mine, she showed us how to peel back the yellow outer skin in order to reach the succulent white fruit beneath.

What immense joy we had over that first banana, I couldn't get over the taste. Never in my life had I been treated to anything like this. It is extraordinary to imagine any child today not knowing what these are and what to do with one when they have it, after all bananas are one of the most common of fruits, on sale everywhere.

The winter of 1946 was extremely cold, every morning we woke to frost patterns on the windows, both inside and out. The air temperature in the bedroom was well below freezing. Coal was expensive and the reserves were guarded very carefully; in our house, these were kept in a kitchen cupboard that was originally designed as a larder. This made sense because, the only fire in the house that was lit, was the little kitchen range. Having the coalhouse in the same room meant that mum didn't have to go outside every time the fire needed making up.

The drawback was that the coalman always came on a Saturday, at lunchtime, when the four of us were at the table. He would come into the room with a full sack on his back then heave the contents into our makeshift coalhouse. The result was always a huge plume of black dust that settled over the food on the plates in front of us. I can tell you now that egg and chips is not improved one little bit by a coating of coal dust. Mr and Mrs Biggs however kept their coal supplies in a bunker outside in the back garden.

Although the bedrooms had open fireplaces, the only time a fire was actually lit in one was if a member of the family was ill, and had to be confined to bed. Only the back kitchen was warm when we woke up in the morning. My mother was a very early riser; her first job, on those extremely cold mornings, was to clear the ashes from the grate from the previous day's fire. This meant taking the ash pan, filled to the brim, right down to the bottom of the garden to empty into the dustbin. Coming back indoors she would sweep out any remaining ashes before taking paper, wood and coal, and lighting the new day's fire.

George and I always had the same routine. First one out of bed had the edge on the other; whoever could grab their clothes and rush downstairs into the kitchen fastest, could claim the chair nearest the fire. Then we would preen over the loser who had to get dressed further away and shiver while he was doing it. Once dressed it was up to the bathroom for teeth cleaning and hands and face wash. Then, quickly back down for a cup of hot tea and a slice of bread, spread with either margarine or beef dripping. We were then ready to start off for another day at Portswood Junior & Infants School.

For some time now trains had been passing the back of our house, filled with men. They waved out of the window to the people who crowded round the railway fence, waving wildly back. These men were all dressed the same, mostly in khaki brown, while some had either dark blue or light blue suits on. These were the uniforms of the army, navy and air force. The cry going up now was that the troops were coming home, but what were troops? And where had they been?

One weekday morning George and I bounded out of bed to start the fire race, as usual. Tearing into the kitchen we stopped dead in absolute horror. The chair nearest the fire, our favourite chair, was not empty. A huge man was sitting in it and looking at us. George's reaction was the same as mine and we both disappeared behind our mother, peeping out at this stranger. Gently she brought us both out into the open and I can hear her now as she said, 'There's nothing for you to be afraid of, this is your father.'

At school we had been learning nursery rhymes, one of which was Jack and the beanstalk. Looking at this big man I was convinced the giant that Jack meets in that rhyme had come down the beanstalk and was now in our house. Corporal William Marsh was just a shade less than 6ft tall and, certainly far from thin, a strongly built man who in fact looked enormous to me. Even though my mother was telling me I had nothing to fear from him, and of course I trusted her completely, I was none the less frightened. Who was this giant? And why was he allowed to pinch our favourite chair?

Formally though mum took both of us by the hand and led us over to our father, who held out his hand and said, 'Hello nippers, it's nice to meet you.' From that day forward my father never referred to any of his sons by their names, we were always 'nipper' to him. He was still wearing his army uniform with two stripes on his arm and I was so confused. Everything my mother or Mrs Biggs said to me I believed because, of course, they were grown-ups and knew what they were talking about. Usually I could make some sort of sense of what they said. But this very large man had come from nowhere. No one had ever told us we had a father.

There had been no excitement the evening before, no news such as 'Daddy's coming home.' The strict Victorian regime to which our parents belonged was still in full force and children were told nothing. So we didn't expect him, he just appeared in our midst. Running to school that day I was to find many children in our year were experiencing the same thing. – complete strangers entering their homes and being told the same, that this is your father. Mrs McGovern tried her best to clarify the situation for us. She told us about the war that had just ended, the part so many men had played in it, and why they had not until now been able to come home. She sternly pointed out how fortunate we were to have our fathers back again, as so many had not come home at all.

This was just about the most confusing time in my life, getting to know this man. I always look back on that day when I held out my small hand and very timidly said, 'How do you do?', to my own father.

# 4

# Monkey Business

It took me some time to get used to the new routine. Ever since my birth there had been two women in charge. We had got used to Ron Biggs but now this giant of a man was with us. But a pattern of life began to assert itself, with my parents now sharing the big front bedroom.

Excitement was just around the corner, because a week after my father's return he went back to the job he had been doing before the war. One day we came home from school to find a lorry parked outside our home. Dad had called in and was just off again, but not before he lifted both George and I up into the cab to show us the controls – this was sensational. The only vehicle either of us had been on, up until now, was a tram, and they were nothing like this. Powered by a petrol-driven engine and not restricted to rails, this lorry could be driven anywhere. The cab was closed in with comfortable seats that were no comparison to the hard wooden ones on the trams.

We were over the moon and it was all mum could do to get us to come in and eat our dinners, much to dad's amusement. We soon learned of his plans to take us out with him on alternate Saturdays. Having a dad suddenly had great advantages and George and I waited, hardly containing our impatience, for the weekend to come when it would be our turn to go out in the lorry.

Sue and Pat had been taken out first, which was only right, because the rule of ladies first was very much recognised at this time. No-one else in Belgrave Road had anything as luxurious as their own motorised transport, so a father with a lorry put us in a most enviable position indeed. Our weekend eventually came and I can recall the thrill of climbing up, with dad's help, into the cab.

We waved wildly to our friends when the engine started. How they must have envied us, and we were already looking forward to seeing their wistful looks when we told them all about this upon our return. We sat enthralled as dad drove us around Southampton, taking in places we had not even heard of before. He stopped at various scrap-metal yards where my brother and I were allowed to play while he was unloading. Just as we thought this day was coming to a close, another wonderful surprise awaited us. The lorry was empty and we went right out of town to a farm to collect some bales of straw. Neither of us had ever seen farm animals before, just domestic dogs and cats. To see sheep, cows and a large bull all roaming free, instead of being led to their deaths in a slaughter house, was a wondrous occasion.

The weekend trips with dad went on for many months and in this way we saw so much more of our shattered town. Southampton was still in ruins; bombed out buildings were everywhere and, indeed, we had already discovered their potential for fun. They made excellent camps and we could play hiding games amongst the rubble or play at Cowboys and Indians or spies using these buildings as our headquarters. Plants were starting to grow within the walls of what had once been family homes or business premises.

We were not allowed to play here because of the safety aspect. Injury, or even death, could be caused by collapsing walls and floors. In respect of this potential hazard the police kept an eye open where ever they could and would chase us out. In those days police officers either walked a beat or patrolled on bicycles. They would warn us off with either a clip round the ear with their bare hand or, and this was much worse, rolled up leather gloves. A few times this happened to me when I didn't run fast enough and boy did it hurt. It was enough to make us keep a close look out every time we played in our bombed-out secret hideouts.

Ours was a small community and everyone pulled together to help with food, clothing or whatever else was needed. Mrs Wilkins came round whenever there was a death, to collect for a wreath. She would knock at every door, never being refused regardless of any financial hardship. The contributions made by each household would be recorded in a little book. So every time a funeral was held for a former resident of Belgrave Road, they were accompanied to the grave by a wreath from all of their friends and neighbours.

Mr Aldridge was the man who had been responsible for defusing an incendiary bomb. He was one of the few people in the whole district to have a telephone in his house. He was also in charge of the Belgrave Church Hall. This was situated on the far side of the bombed buildings and was used by various groups and for different events, from the Girl's Friendly Society (GFS) to whist drives for the adults. This hall was a subsidiary of the very beautiful South Stoneham Church.

Whenever anyone went into hospital Mr Aldridge would ring up every day to find out how they were. He would then post a bulletin on the church hall door, so that anyone who wanted to know could come and chart their progress. This was a service he did for many years, sometimes with very sad outcomes, and we were grateful to him for the trouble he took to provide it.

On many occasions, when money was really short, George and I went down there if we needed a haircut. This was always done in the back-garden shed. Not the most enjoyable thing for either of us; Mr Aldridge had his own idea of short back and sides, and it certainly wasn't anything like a real barber would have done. We also had to face the rest of our respective gangs afterwards and none of them were ever sympathetic to our plight. But it was free and it helped mum, so we had to put up with it. The only consolation to this ordeal, that I can bring to mind, was that the Aldridge family kept rabbits.; so at least we had these to look at while our hair was being butchered.

As we all had coal fires the chimneys had to be swept at least once a year. On our road we had our own chimney sweep in residence; Mr Noyce lived right down the bottom end in No.6. I remember running down to his house, knocking at the door and telling him, 'Mummy would like her chimney swept.'

Later on that same day we would be standing in the road waiting for the first sign of the brush as it popped out the top of the chimney. Then either George or I, sometimes both of us together, would rush indoors and let the sweep know. The brush had to go all the way up and sections were screwed on, making it longer and longer. Then the skill of the sweep really came into play as he brought the brush back down and with it all the soot that had built up over a long period of time, without making a huge mess inside the house. Mr Noyce achieved this by wrapping large cloths around the front of the kitchen range. The soot fell behind this and he then swept it into sacks to be disposed of safely.

We were all very wary of 'Tykie' McArthur. This was the name my parents and all the adults in the road had given him. We were taught to respect our elders so to us, at least to his face, he was Mr McArthur. Tykie's house stood out from the rest of the road for so many reasons. The front door was almost always wide open and walking past, it was impossible not to notice the gaps in the floorboards. These were caused by Tykie himself; whenever they were short of wood for fuel he would prise up a floorboard and use that. Inside there were doors missing as well, these having suffered the same fate. This practice dated back to the depression of the 1920s where so many extremely hard up families survived by doing things like this. Tykie, however, had never got out of the habit.

All the Belgrave children knew their way around the back cut ways by now. One of these, on the opposite side of the road from our house, led past the back of the McArthur home. The back yard had nothing growing in it, but he did have a donkey, two goats and at least six dogs. These were kept in one large wooden kennel and we never saw them when they were inside. Sometimes they would escape, erupting through the house into the centre of the road – always led by a huge jet-black mongrel, who had them fighting furiously with each other, and making a fearful noise. What frightened us even more was when Mr McArthur appeared brandishing a whip. with this he lashed out at the dogs, roaring at the top of his voice until they fled in terror back to the safety of the kennel. I never fail to see Tykie and his whip every time I look back on those days.

He was not a bad man, far from it. He, like all his neighbours, would give his last slice of bread to anyone he thought needed it more than him. Another thing we certainly didn't know about this remarkable man was that Tykie took in unmarried mothers. In the forties and fifties a woman having a baby out of wedlock was an absolute disgrace. Families often disowned girls who became pregnant while still single. So girls in this predicament had nowhere to go and no-one to turn to. Out of the goodness of his heart he took them into his home, allowing them to stay until their babies were born. That was the kind of man he was. But of course we knew nothing about this and wouldn't have understood if we had been told.

Belgrave Road had its quota of underprivileged people and these were accepted without prejudice by everyone. We had at least four who we described as 'backward', the correct term today being people with learning difficulties. Three of them were grown-ups, but had the minds of children our age. Indeed one of them was known as 'Chickie' but his real name was John. He joined in our games on so many occasions. Even though the age gap was so great, not one of us thought it odd that Chickie should want to play with us.

The other person we knew well was Edwin Whelan's younger brother Kenny. Even the hard men of our gang, namely Pat Marriot and Timmy Donaldson, never laughed or made fun of Kenny. In fact they did just the opposite and would sit and talk with him for ages, and accepted him as just another Belgrave boy. He couldn't communicate with us on our own level, but we liked him none the less. Our parents all respected Mr and Mrs Whelan for the way they diligently looked after their youngest son. They could have sent him to an institution but instead they made sure Kenny had as near a normal upbringing in a caring family, as it was possible to give him.

Ray Broadbent lived just two doors down from us at No.90 and was one of three brothers. The eldest of these we hardly knew at all but Ray and his brother, David, played with us. David, like all of us, was completely able-bodied. Ray however had suffered from polio as a child and, as a result, was crippled, having to walk with the aid of two sticks. Describing him as crippled is really an insult to him because he could keep up with us quite easily wherever we went and whatever distance we travelled. We never had to stop to let him catch up.

When playing football in the road, the secret was to be picked to play on the same side as Ray. To play against him was definitely hazardous. He couldn't use his feet, so he substituted his sticks. Reaching the ball he would lash out with one or the other, depending on which side of him it had fallen. Anyone foolish enough to try and tackle Ray would find one of them descending at speed and with agonising effect, landing across either their knees or shins. Just about every mother in Belgrave Road at one time or another had to comfort a sobbing son who had just been whacked by one of Ray Broadbent's sticks.

Christmas of 1946 far surpassed the one we had known the year before. To start with we had a father, and we now knew all about Jesus, and what this great festival was really about. At school we learned our lines and put on a nativity play in front of our parents. This was both a joy and a disaster. I played a shepherd, dressed up in long robes from a box that Mrs McGovern kept for this performance each year.

Standing innocently in a field, I was tending my sheep when the angel of the Lord, played by Bobby Westmore, was lowered down. Unfortunately the rope broke before his feet touched the floor. Gallantly Pat Marriot, Edwin Whelan and I rushed to help as he was now hanging precariously half on and half off the stage. Somehow my shepherd's crook became entangled between Edwin's legs, tripping him up so he cannoned into Pat, pushing him into me. All of us, Bobby included, ended up on the floor, to the howling amusement of our parents, and the glaring disapproval of Mrs McGovern.

Picking ourselves up, we sorted out our now broken shepherds crooks, and returned to the makeshift field to be told a king was born to us this day. Although not the most successful performance I think we managed to show we knew what Christmas was all about.

At home the decorations went up again, turning the house into a fairy grotto. Early on the morning of Christmas Eve, mum went up to Martin's the butcher to pick out our one great treat of the year, a turkey. By the time we got up that morning, this magnificent bird was already lying in what served as a fridge – the bathtub – when not in use, in the winter, it was extremely cold. The turkey was placed there throughout the day, ready to be put in the oven early on Christmas morning for that special dinner. Every time we trooped up the stairs we would gaze into the bathroom in awe.

All sorts of goodies arrived during the day as mum went again and again to the shops, bringing back sweets, cakes, fizzy drinks, and other things we didn't normally get during the year. This was not easy for her as rationing was still so strict, but help was at hand. There were two small shops in Belgrave Road.

One of these was a conventional corner shop, known to us all as Harold Brown's, owned and run by a very congenial man, Mr Brown. He knew all the families in the road and would help out, especially at times like Christmas. Nothing illegal, just a few extra things sold to individuals without taking the coupons. This helped make the food go around in so many homes. Everyone who knew Harold Brown respected and liked him for the help he gave. This extended to the children as well and we always stopped and talked to him as we passed on our various journeys.

The other place was very different. This was Johnnie Fryer's, just across the road from us. He had turned the front room of his house into a shop. We would go through the front door to be confronted by a bench that served as a counter. Shouting 'shop' at the top of our voices would bring Mr Fryer shuffling out of his back room. Describing this man is not easy because we did not like him at all. There was something menacing that we all detected and shied away from. He was a short thin man with a fierce pinched face, and he would glare at us and snap, 'Yes. What do you want?' He was in fact the complete opposite of Harold Brown.

In answer to this demand we would timidly hand him the list our mothers had given us. Snatching these from us he would first scan them before disappearing under the counter to fetch the various contents. Where he got his stock from I never found out, but I now know he had things that regular traders couldn't get. We knew nothing about the black market but that was the most probable source of this man's supplies. We never had to take ration books with us whenever we were sent to shop at Fryer's. It may have been a great help to our parents having somewhere like this where sugar, butter, and other perishables were cheaper and free from coupons, but for us it was always an ordeal.

All the food, clothing and every other essential item that was bought during the year were ticked up. We never had enough money to get what was needed so it was buy now and pay later. In its way this was an early version of today's credit cards, except our mothers didn't have a small piece of plastic, just a little book, into which everything that was owed was listed. At the end of each week, when mum was given her housekeeping money, she paid it all out to the various shop keepers until there was nothing left. So, it was back to ticking up for the following weeks provisions. Christmas was expensive and always went on a separate account that usually took almost all of the next year to pay off. Still our parents put themselves out, my mother in particular often going without herself, to see that special occasions were provided for.

On Christmas Day George and I had woken up at around five o'clock in the morning, and dived to the bottom of our beds to gleefully look at what Father Christmas had brought us; and what a treat there was. I had a large model car as a main present, along with a book, the ever-present plasticine, and another jigsaw. A larger one this time, and of course I now knew what to do with it. As soon as we were allowed we ran out into the road, eagerly showing our friends what we had this year, and also seeing what they had got on this special day.

Dad was home and it was he who cooked the wonderful Christmas dinner. He was a great cook and the meal was good enough to have been served in a restaurant. It started with his unbelievable giblet soup. This was the first time we had anything other than mulligatawny. The giblets were boiled for twenty-four hours before being strained and a tomato cube added. The result was a soup that, I, for one, would have been content to have even more helpings of.

There were also Aunty Ada's homemade Christmas puddings that were no comparison at all to the large bulky suet ones mum made for us during the year. These were extremely filling, sometimes being made with fruit and called 'spotted dick' as a result. Other times they were plain and we put a small amount of precious sugar on them. Because they were so filling these regular puddings helped to make up for the shortages of food in other departments. The Christmas puddings however were special because they contained many ingredients that made them taste different from my mother's.

Mother had been brought up in a strict Victorian regime, and naturally kept to the principles she had been taught by her grandmother. This was that, the man of the house, was the most important member. It was he who went out to work, brought in the money that went to the upkeep, and took care of the needs of the entire family. Therefore, he was to be treated with the utmost respect and was not to be burdened with children. Because of this we never really had the chance to get to know our father properly. He was isolated from us and we never sat down to a meal at the same time. It was children first and grown-ups afterwards.

As soon as dad set foot in the house from work it was the signal for all of us to be shooed out to play, either in the road, or, if it was wet or dark outside, in the small hall just inside the front door. I can see him now, walking over to the coalhouse door and hanging his cap on the hook placed there for this purpose. A solitary figure sitting alone at the table – my mother never joined him. She had already eaten her small portion of meagre pickings, as she served everyone else's meals. No, the family bread winner ate alone before moving to the chair nearest the kitchen range to read the evening newspaper. My mother's huge contributions to the household, the shopping, cleaning, cooking, as well as looking after all of us, were not even taken into consideration.

Christmas was different in one respect. This time mum would join dad in the Brook Inn at lunch time, making sure we ate a very large dinner before leaving us in the charge of Mrs Biggs. On returning home she would join dad at the table and eat hers, the only time she ever did this. We wondered how on earth she survived and I put it down to another thing she got from great-grandmother. We often had cabbage with our dinners and I for one never complained about this because I actually liked it. Every time mum cooked cabbage she would pour off a cup full of the water it was boiled in and drink this. All the goodness from the vegetables, especially the green root ones, goes into the water during the cooking process. Drinking it by the cupful she benefited from these vitamins and kept herself going, even though it must have tasted awful. She sacrificed so much so that her family remained clothed and fed, and I am so proud of her for that.

Birthdays were another occasion when enormous sacrifices were made. Each of us were given a party with cakes, jelly and custard, and as many sweets as she could afford and had the ration coupons for. Those parties were attended by all the family as well as a few close friends. In my case this usually meant Edwin Whelan, Pat Marriot, Dave Simmons, Bobby Westmore and John Bates, as well as some of the girls.

Always present here was Vickie Masterman. She was so pretty, with her long dark hair and I felt excitement whenever I was with her, but didn't understand this. Because the boy-girl divide was so strong, we were told absolutely nothing about the feelings girls and boys have for one another. Sex was definitely never mentioned in public; even ladies underwear was considered totally unmentionable, especially if any children were around. The other girls I liked and enjoyed playing with, but I saw them as great friends and part-time members of the Belgrave Road gang. Vickie though was always special ,and, was in fact, the very first love of my life.

For me 1947 was a memorable year and it began with an unexpected holiday from school. British winters in those days were very cold but this one was even more so. The roads became frozen over with thick layers of ice. A joy for us, as we were able to make slides on the pavements, much to the disapproval of our parents, as they were then a danger to everyone else. We rushed along gaining speed before leaping in the air and landing hard, sliding for long distances. This left great slippery lines that the grown-ups had to be careful to avoid.

Then an unbelievable thing happened. Mrs McGovern came into the classroom to tell us we could all go home because the schools pipes had frozen solid, and there was now no water in either the washrooms or toilets. We were deliriously happy to have an extra unexpected holiday. My mother, however, was not so pleased to see us home. While we were at school we were out of her way and the routine was always the same. She was so proud of her home and cleaned it from top to bottom six days a week. On Sundays, after she had spent the morning cooking and serving the roast dinner, she would get us on our way to Sunday school, before spending, that one afternoon ,relaxing and listening to her favourite radio programmes.

Children were not wanted in the house when this weekly cleaning was in progress. We were always shooed out whenever there was a danger of us being in the way. Even in the worst rain storms it was, 'Right you kids, out.'. Out we had to go; even if we told her it was pouring down with rain, she would still tell us, 'Go and shelter under the cut, but get outside out of the way.' By this, she meant that we could go and huddle under the covered part of the cut that led up to the tram stop, outside Lock's fish and chip shop, in Portswood Road.

Inside the house mum would already be moving the furniture in the kitchen over to one side of the room, before dusting the now-exposed part of the floor. Then, getting down on her hands and knees, she would polish the lino using a round tin called Ronuck. When the lino gleamed to her satisfaction she would replace the furniture to that side of the room, followed by all the rest from the opposite side. Then the dusting and polishing were repeated. The very last thing she wanted while this was being done was a tribe of kids under her feet.

She needn't have worried on this occasion, however. It had snowed heavily during the night and we couldn't wait to get out into the road. Everyone was there, the girls as well, and the cold meant nothing to us as we formed two groups and started snowball fights. There were also contests to see who could build the biggest snowmen on the bombed buildings. A lot of skulduggery went on here though, as snowmen mysteriously fell over, just as they were taking shape. This could not, of course, have had anything to do with the three biggest rascals in the road – Pat Marriot, John Bates and Timmy Donaldson – could it?

A great time was had by all of us during that glorious unscheduled holiday, resulting in chapped hands and chilblains on the soles of our feet. The traditional remedy for this was camphorated oil. This came in little bottles which were warmed in front of the fire. When heated sufficiently this was applied to the offending parts of our bodies, including our chests, which were rubbed vigorously to prevent colds and chills. In most cases it worked fine, although we didn't like it at all. Like everything else, including being rubbed raw in the bath, it was applied with such a large amount of vigour that, it left us gasping for breath afterwards.

This though was nothing compared to the fate awaiting us on our return to school. We met that paragon of dread, the school nurse, who brought with her a bottle of evil smelling liquid and a metal comb. This was the nit lady and we were about to enter her chamber of horrors. Being led up we were bent forward so she could grasp our heads before applying this chemical that made us gag with its awful smell. But worse was still to come as she applied that metal comb, scraping it through our hair while pressing down hard on our scalp. This action was repeated several times, despite our loud cries, to make sure there were no nits in our hair.

What was this mad woman talking about? What were nits? And why did we have to suffer in this way? Our mothers had to be present with us at the school before this examination could take place. Eventually we were let go, but not before they were shown how to do the same thing at home, to keep up a regular vigil against head lice.

At home we were told dad had gone away again for a few weeks. He had left his job as a lorry driver, much to the disgust of Sue, Pat, George and I, and sailed on one of the Union Castle liners. These came and went each week from Southampton to South Africa. The fun started when he returned six weeks later. He had been using the Newlands Hotel a lot before he went away and we liked to go across there because this public house had something that excited us very much, a menagerie in the garden. Not only were we allowed to have lemonade and sometimes a packet of crisps each, we could see animals that we had only previously heard about.

The pub was run by a man we knew by the affectionate title of Uncle Wally, and we all liked him so much. He welcomed us and loved to watch as we spent ages amongst his animals. He only had one monkey, and, although we were very pleased to see this cute and cuddly thing, none of us knew he was lonely. When dad found out, he took it on himself to bring a female monkey back from South Africa, as a companion to Uncle Wally's lonely male. How he got away with it I will never know; considering how strict the quarantine laws are, and were even then, in this country. But it was just after the war, and the police had other things to occupy them.

In order to get the monkey through customs my father hatched a plot, involving two dolls. He had bought one each for both Sue and Pat, who incidentally he always referred to as Ginny, short for Ginny Maria. So he had the dolls in two separate boxes but also obtained an identical empty one. Coming through customs in Southampton on his return to this country, he had these boxes tied together with a doll in both the top and bottom ones, and a live monkey in the middle. To the custom's officials question, as to the contents of the boxes, dad simply said, 'three dolls.' Incredibly he was believed and passed through safely. However, once in a taxi and on his way home, the driver asked the same question then pointed out that the one in the middle was very lifelike and extremely active.

Horrified, my father looked and saw that the monkey had somehow managed to tear a hole in its box, pushed its arm through and it was hanging on to the string that held all three boxes together. If that had happened while he was going through customs he would have had some very awkward questions to answer. But he made it home and, after greeting my mother and all of his children, he gave George and me the presents he had brought home for us, as well as a wonderfully juicy and delicious Cape orange each. He had brought a whole sack of these back with him, which was an unbelievable treat for the whole family.

At the same time mum was opening the dolls to give to the girls. When dad saw this he yelled a warning but it was too late. With a shriek of alarm mum leapt back as a brown, and very lively monkey, jumped out and streaked straight up the curtains of the kitchen window. There was no time for explanations. It had to be recaptured and we were all pressed into service. The monkey however was free and it had every intention of remaining that way.

Despite our superior numbers that small furry animal led us on a mad rush around most of the house. No one in those days, especially not from our working class background, had television. They were far out of the price range of our parents and were therefore only to be found in the houses of very posh people. What we had for home entertainment was a wireless, a funny name for something that had wires coming out of it in all directions. An earth wire went from the back of the set out the window and was pushed into the ground through a hole in the concrete. But the power for the set came from the one that was plugged into the light socket next to the electric light bulb.

The monkey of course used this with eye-blinking speed. Each time it came into the kitchen it leaped onto this wire and swung effortlessly over our heads. With a horrible groaning noise the wireless started to lurch back and plunged to the floor. We all dived to catch it, George and I getting in each other's way, but we couldn't prevent it from hitting the floor with a very big bang indeed.

With everyone in pursuit, the monkey rushed up the stairs. In and out of the bedrooms, the chase went on, now joined by Mrs Biggs who had come out of her room to see what all the noise was about. Out of the bathroom and back down the stairs went the monkey, knocking over the copper tub mum used to do all of the family's washing. A lot of this was inside at the time so the mess this made was terrible. But the monkey went on evading the outstretched arms that were trying so hard to catch it.

It was Blitz the cat who eventually brought the great chase to a successful conclusion. She had at first fled in terror at the sight of this strange creature in the house. Now though, in the middle of all the uproar, she decided to stand her ground. After all, this was her house and no other animal was welcome. So she suddenly threw herself into the path of the monkey as it flew along the floor, heading once more for the kitchen. Her back arched, she let out a loud hissing noise while lashing out with her paw.

The monkey was taken completely by surprise, as we all were, and it stopped dead in front of this obvious threat. We were near enough to take advantage of it, and it was Mrs Biggs who threw a coat over the fugitive, allowing dad to scoop it up. Then, before my mother could give vent at the near destruction of her beautiful home – by the alien creature – he went straight out of the door, shouting that he was taking it to Wally, at the Newlands.

# 5

# I Do Like To Be Beside the Seaside

Dad had the good sense to stay at the pub long enough to give my mother a chance to clean up the mess. The wireless no longer worked. In those days they had a series of valves inside, some of which had been broken in the fall, not to mention the crack in the casing. The copper in the scullery was put upright again but we were all shooed out of the house as the big clean up began.

Uncle Wally got his second monkey, much to the relief of the lone one already in residence. Dad, as well as having a lot of explaining to do to my irate mother, had to somehow replace the radio with the minimum of delay. To say that my mother relied on this is a huge understatement. Her day quite literally revolved around it. From the time she got up in the morning until going to bed at night it was on. She loved to listen to plays and music shows, and her two top favourites were Women's Hour and Mrs Dale's Diary. For these she actually stopped work and sat down to listen. Without the radio her days were an oasis of emptiness as she worked in a silence that was alien to her.

The problem was partly solved by going next door to No.92. Here the Golden family lived and she could listen to those two shows with them. For us there was only one worry, the program that came on at seven o'clock each evening. This was *Dick Barton Special Agent*. Every evening all the children in the road, the girls as well as the boys, disappeared indoors to listen with bated breath as Dick faced an endless trail of hair raising adventures. We sat by the set and gasped as he was in danger, then cheered when he managed to triumph. Up and down the country children in their millions listened every night to this serial.

So during our radio crisis I went to the house of Edwin Whelan and listened with him and his sister. After which we ran out to play again until our parents came out to call us in at bedtime. We pleaded for 'just five more minutes' and we always got it. I think this request was anticipated and we were called five minutes early so that it could be granted with no loss of face, although we thought we were being crafty. Two weeks after our original wireless was broken, dad replaced it with another he got second hand, this was installed just before he went back to sea. Where this other wireless came from no one asked, but peace was restored, my mother pacified, and the monkey episode faded into memory.

By this time I had turned into what I can only describe as a spoilt little brat. I found that as I was the youngest I could get away with anything. No matter what I did, if it went wrong either Sue, Pat or George got the blame for it, with a firm clout on either the arms or legs, which really stung. Then, adding insult to injury, they were sat in a chair, forbidden to move and roared at by mum, 'Now you sit there and don't move, and don't you dare cry.'

The more I realised they would be blamed for my misdeeds the worse I became. I would play with things I wasn't supposed to touch, like coal, getting large lumps out of the coalhouse and arranging it in piles on the kitchen floor – getting filthy in the process. All the toys we had between us were kept neatly stacked away in a cardboard box when not in use. I would take them out and scatter them all over the place – in the house as well as out in the garden – so they were in everyone's way, which of course infuriated my fastidious mother.

I knocked over and broke essential things like crockery that was difficult to replace. The worse I got the more my sisters and brother suffered. Mum always accompanied the slaps by saying, 'You're all older than him and you should have been watching.' This was unfair, as I was much too fast for them and this was never more evident than the day we went to the recreation ground on the other side of Portswood Senior School.

There was a very wide area of fields and tennis courts, a slide, roundabouts, two see-saws and several swings. Needless to say most of our time, especially in our infancy, was spent here, and we were not careful about what we did. Our favourite pastime was to get the roundabout spinning as fast as we could then see who was brave enough to try and jump on. It was a long time before I tried this as I saw more than one boy do it, only to be thrown off again with alarming results.

Sue, Pat and George, as well as enjoying themselves, also had the job of looking after me. But naturally with all of their friends there they couldn't always be watching to see what I was doing. I was fascinated by the swings. Not sitting on them and seeing how high I could make them go, but running in between them while they were swinging backwards and forwards. Boys and girls were shrieking with fun and sometimes fright as they were swept into the air and swiftly back down again, so took no notice at all of a silly little boy.

Inevitably I got it all wrong and ran forward just as one of the swings was coming back, hitting me with a bang across my forehead. I was knocked completely off my feet and sent back in a sprawling heap to land several yards away. My head was cut open and blood ran down my face as a horrified Sue, followed closely by the others came running up. There were several of the Belgrave gang there that day and they rushed off at once to alert my mother, as well as their own, that little Jimmy Marsh had been hurt.

I had by this time been lifted into the arms of one of the men of Brickfield Road and carried home, accompanied by a very worried Pat and George. Sue had realised the gravity of the situation and measured the punishment likely to be meted out. So she ran off to hide, coming home much later on to everyone's concern. It did her no good because she still got a hiding from mum. As for me, as soon as I came in sight of Belgrave I was snatched up by all the women of the road, who had been alerted to this crisis. After thanking the man who had carried me this far I was rushed indoors for emergency first aid.

Everyone's home was an open house in those days. Most families kept a key on a piece of string which was dangled down inside the front door. If you needed to gain entrance for any reason you only had to push open the letter box and reach inside for the string. Our house had the key permanently in the lock so anyone could turn it and open the door whenever they wanted. Despite this, I never knew of anyone who abused this system by overstaying their welcome. Nor did I know of any house in this remarkable road that ever got burgled. This present situation was seen as an emergency, which meant many of my friend's mothers crowded into our home to offer help and comfort.

Remarkably I hadn't been hurt as badly as everyone thought. It was just a deep cut and bruising and I was taken into the room that usually was forbidden territory. This was the downstairs living room of Mr and Mrs Biggs. Here I had to endure a great deal of pain and discomfort as Mrs Biggs bathed the cut on my head and applied a bandage soaked in iodine, which really stung. She then cleaned the scratches and placed a poultice on the bruises. Through all my tears she told me what a brave little boy I was for sitting still and allowing her to do it. To my eye popping amazement I was given a reward, a plate of biscuits.

Instantly I forgot all about my injuries as I looked at this wonderful array. They weren't the plain variety mum always bought for us, these were cream biscuits. Once more I have to say this was a first. I had never seen any like this before with custard cream. The only way any of us would get near something as luxurious as cream biscuits was to be an accident victim.

While I was in Mrs Biggs' room being treated like a prince I could hear my mother's voice rise in anger and this was directed at Pat and George, 'Why did it happen?' she yelled and I heard the sound of a slap. 'Why weren't you watching him? He could have been killed.' Being the smug little wretch that I was, I laughed to myself as I heard more slaps being administered and was hugely enjoying their downfall.

Outside the house things were very different. Here I was just another member of the Belgrave gang and treated the same as every boy and girl there. None of our fathers earned enough to properly meet the demands of a growing family so everyone struggled to make ends meet. This meant pocket money was out of the question, so we had to find ways and means of earning our own. This was done in different ways, the first of which was running errands. We knew the whereabouts of the various shops in our own area and would run back and forth between these for anyone who wanted something.

Getting the orders right was very important, as was the correct change. For each successfully completed errand we were rewarded with 3*d*, a good rate of pay when you consider the responsibility that was accepted by us on a daily basis. The ration books were so important. Everything these people needed over a three month period was covered by the coupons in them. If we lost them then the family concerned would be in very dire straits indeed. Money alone would not do it so this part of the operation was of vital importance. None of us ever suffered the terrible consequences this would have brought. We made sure those ration books were placed safely in the bags with the produce and in this way safely returned to their owners.

Another source of revenue was empty beer bottles, which were returned to one or other of the two local pubs, the Newlands Hotel or the Brook Inn. It was easier for us to take these to the Brook, providing they had come from there or any one of the other Marstons' houses in the area. There was a little room at the front known as the 'bottle and jug'. As children we were allowed in here and so, when we had a few bottles we would crowd in and plonk them onto the little counter. The bar staff would count them and give us the refundable deposits our fathers had paid as part of the price for the full bottle. This was a very satisfactory means of revenue because for each bottle returned in this way we received 3*d*. So to be able to take four back meant we got the enormous sum of 1*s*.

We discovered very early on a little yard in Priory Road that took jam jars. So every now and again we went round to the houses and shops in our area asking for these. When we had collected as many as we could, we would borrow a pram from one of our homes and use this to transport the jars to the yard. The man in charge would line them up in two rows for counting. He walked up in between, counting them as he went with all of us keeping pace and watching him like a hawk. The price was a halfpenny each, and we always knew how many we had brought and just how much we should be paid, so there was no cheating on either side.

Money for everyone was extremely scarce so large gardens were used to grow vegetables. Potatoes, runner beans, carrots, peas, cabbages, and onions were all cultivated to supplement the family budget. For this venture to be successful it was necessary to use fertilizer. Unfortunately there was nowhere for anyone to buy this, even if they could have afforded the purchase price. Certainly as far as I remember none of the shops in Southampton sold anything so luxurious. To solve this problem most gardeners turned to nature's natural remedy, namely horse manure.

This we could get because in the forties, most of the roundsmen, who delivered things like milk, bread etc., used horse-drawn carts. We particularly liked the milkman. As well as being allowed to feed the horse a slice of bread, he always let us ride up on the milk cart all the way along Belgrave Road. We got to know that horse and the animal knew the round as well as his driver. He always stopped in the right places so that the milkman could deliver as he went along. This was particularly useful at Christmas when the milk man was invited in. Most of the housewives gave him a drink of sherry, as well as a small tip, so he got drunk as he went along. Somehow he managed to climb back up onto the cart and the horse simply plodded on to the next stop.

The manure was collected by teams of boys following the horses as they went from street to street, armed with a bucket and shovel. As soon as the horse answered the call of nature, the following boys would swoop and shovel the manure into their buckets, often in dispute with boys from other roads who were out on the same mission. It became simply a straight race to see who could run the fastest and get there first. This precious manure was sold for the princely sum of 6d a bucket and was a good source of income. This was enough to buy sweets to share among us all.

There were of course other special occasions such as Guy Fawkes Night. We all went out with our homemade guys and did very well indeed. The money gained was spent on fireworks which were let off on this glorious night. There was also carol singing at Christmas. In our own way, and through our own devices, we had pocket money but it was used sparingly.

We now knew our way around Southampton and had targeted many of the bomb sites as our own playground. Edwin Whelan and I found our way to the old walls that had once surrounded this ancient south-coast town. Exploring these in great excitement we came to a point that overlooked the factory of Pirelli General Cable Works. Walking these walls was just like being in a castle and this particular part had a round tower underneath which to our great delight was a dungeon. On top of this tower we had the pleasure of playing with the mounting that had once held an anti-aircraft gun used to fire at marauding German planes during the recent war.

Uncle Wally, who still ran the Newlands Hotel, realised all the children who came into his garden had never been on any sort of trip. All of us were war babies and had travelled nowhere, as most vehicles were commandeered by the armed forces. Now we were being told he had arranged an outing to Bournemouth, a place none of us had even heard of. This is a town roughly 30 miles from Southampton and reached by travelling through the beauty of the New Forest. This was explained to us a week before and I was fascinated by the tales I was hearing about the seaside. I couldn't wait and had trouble sleeping the night before.

We were to travel in something my mother referred to as a charabanc. I had no idea what this was but when eight of them arrived together in Belgrave Road I could hardly contain myself. Today they are better known as a coach, and when I first went inside I was speechless. I had travelled many miles by tram and enjoyed the luxury of trips in my father's lorry; but this vehicle had seats facing the same way which were extremely comfortable to sit in, large windows and went along faster than anything I had travelled in.

The huge panorama of the New Forest, the pride and joy of the county of Hampshire, was breathtaking and an awesome experience for us all. We could hardly believe the scenes as they raced by the windows. From the tree-covered forest to wide open plains, this area was simply beautiful, especially the sight of the many ponies roaming free. Soon though most of the grown-ups started singing 'I Do Like To Be Beside the Seaside.'

I will never forget my first sight of the open sea, pointed out to all of us as we came in sight of it. Even from the windows it filled me with excitement. The procession of eight charabancs, of which ours was bringing up the rear, pulled up on the promenade at Bournemouth. I could see and smell the saltwater and I wanted to get as close to it as possible. So, as soon as my feet touched solid ground I was off.

I ran towards the beach threading my little body through the masses of people who were enjoying their day out. Finally reaching the place where the waves came crashing up the shore, these went straight over my shoes and socks but this didn't bother me one bit. I was so excited, so enthralled by this, and turned to run back and tell mum how wonderful it was. The trouble was I had no idea where she was, I had rushed off so quickly and passed so many people in my quest to reach the sea. Now as I looked around, in growing despair, I saw complete strangers around me. I was in a panic now and burst into tears as my predicament became clear. Fortunately a kindly group of mothers were there with their own children and came up to find out what was wrong.

Tearfully blurting out, 'I can't find my mummy,' they summoned a policeman who took me kindly by the hand and led me to the lost children's hut on the promenade. I had been taught by then, both at home and at school, to state my name and address if I was ever lost, and so was able to give this information to the people in charge. This resulted in a loud speaker announcement asking Mrs Marsh of Belgrave Road, Southampton, to come to the hut on the promenade, where her son Jimmy was waiting for her. This was received with some relief by mum and the rest of our group, who by then were dividing themselves up into search parties to go and look for me.

Mum duly collected me and her relief soon turned to anger at the silly way I had run off. 'Don't do it again,' she admonished me and I made sure I never did. As soon as I was reunited with my family, Uncle Wally came up and said to mum he would like to take a photograph of our family group, 'Before this little shaver gets himself lost again,' he said, playfully ruffling my hair. I still have that photo, taken so long ago on Bournemouth beach. Not only do I cherish the memory of it, I am convinced that seeing the sea that day started a love of everything and anything to do with it.

Later that year, when I was still a month short of my seventh birthday, I went with mum to a woman's meeting she always attended, and did for a number of years afterwards. This was held on Thursday afternoon in Portswood's Hebren Hall, now known as Portswood Church, at the far end of the junction. If we were home from school with no-one available to look after us we had to trail along. Usually we were looked after in the nursery. This wasn't so bad, there were always toys to play with and other children to either share or fight with over possession of these playthings.

On this particular day however the nursery was closed and, much to my disgust, I had to go into the hall with my mother and sit quietly and still while hymns were sung. Then the guest speaker would spend at least half an hour, a lifetime for me, giving a lecture on one subject or another. I was firmly convinced there should have been a law against this because a boy of my age just wanted to be running around all the time.

This time though the speaker's subject was the *Titanic*. Coming from Southampton, seeing huge liners was nearly an everyday occurrence. But this ship, which had sailed from the White Star Dock on 10 April 1912, the same year incidentally that my father was born, was thought to be unsinkable. I listened and was totally fascinated by the story, how it hit an iceberg and sank during the night with the loss of 1,500 lives. I even conquered the shyness I felt when in the company of strangers and timidly went up to the lecturer to ask about the captain. I was told this was Edward J. Smith who was the Commodore of the White Star Line, and went down with the ship.

I have, in consequence, had a lifetime of interest in the *Titanic*. I have several books on the subject and have read over and over again how the tragedy affected Southampton. Most of the 680 or so crew who died came from this seaport, indeed two members of that ship's crew came from Belgrave, so even the greatest of all sea disasters affected our little road.

During the school year of 1947/48 we came to know and associate with a boy from our class who lived in an enormous house on the corner of Broadlands Road. His name was Roger Mordingham and all of the Belgrave Gang, with the exception of Edwin Whelan, played here. Compared to the size of the houses we lived in this was unbelievably large. There were three floors and the one at the top had four different attic rooms, all empty and available to us. This was far beyond our wildest dreams and beat our bombsite playgrounds with some ease.

Here on the top floor of this safe and private house we had our spy headquarters, pirate stronghold and a sheriff's office and jail. When the weather was good we went outside to play, either in the large back garden, or rolling down the sloping lawns at the front. Quite why Edwin didn't play in this house with us I don't know, but the rest of us had the time of our lives.

Christmas of 1947 was memorable because we saw, for the first time, the most enormous tree. We had never seen one inside a house before. It was set up in the large front lounge and was decorated with all sorts of things. But what fascinated me were the fairy lights that sparkled in different colours. There was something for everyone on that tree. As so many of us were there we certainly didn't expect presents. I was speechless when Mrs Mordingham handed me a large toy snowman and then showed me how to open it by removing its head. Inside were crammed sweets of all different varieties.

In early 1948 the Mordingham family moved away and the great house fell empty. But not before the day we decided to dig our way through to a country our new teacher at Portswood School, Mr Duncan, had told us about. Australia was on the opposite side of the world and it seemed reasonable to assume if we dug a large enough hole, we would eventually come out there. We would have a quick look around, allowing enough time for the return journey to the Mordingham garden to get home for our tea. This was always at four thirty and definitely not to be missed.

While the digging was underway using tools found in the garden shed, it all went horribly wrong. John Bates raised a garden fork over his head, before bringing it down hard in order to dig out more dirt. But he got it wrong and instead of going into the earth, the prongs of the fork went straight through his foot. Not surprisingly excavations came to an abrupt halt as we tried frantically to get help. I can still see Pat Marriot suffused with laughter as he watched John screaming with pain and squirming around trying to pull the fork out of his foot. But even he quickly realised the seriousness of this situation and the laughter abruptly stopped as he became as worried as the rest of us. Fortunately help soon arrived and the grown-ups took over. John was rushed to hospital where he remained for quite some time.

We also played alongside the railway line that went past Belgrave Road, having been warned on many occasions of the dangers. A story was told of a boy who was hit by a train, losing one of his legs as a consequence. So the message was clear, stay off the line. This we all heeded but got up to some tricks of our own anyway.

The dare, from Pat Marriot of course, was to see who was brave enough to sit behind a bush right at the top of the railway bank and stay there as one of the many express trains to London thundered by just feet away. The first time I actually did this I was petrified. The noise of the steam engine and the rattle of the carriage wheels made my head spin and I thought the end of the world had come. Amazingly though I grew used to it and before long found this practice quite tame.

I loved to forage around the grassy area between the railway bank and the fence to look for glow worms. They might have fascinated me, but certainly made no impression at all on the female members of the Marsh family. I was told in no uncertain manner to 'Take those nasty things back where you found them.' While looking for these however we had to sort through mounds of rubbish that had been thrown away over a long period of time. It was a very handy dumping place for anything you had no more use for and that couldn't be handed on to anyone else.

Edwin Whelan had no interest in glow worms, but was very excited when he was given an authentic Victorian Hoop, the kind you bowled along with a stick. At first we took turns with this and ran it up and down the road. But one wasn't nearly enough as we waited impatiently for our turn. It was Bobby Westmore who hit on the idea of using the many damaged bicycle wheels lying around the railway dump. These wheels all had very bent spokes, but with our father's help they were removed, leaving us with the perfectly shaped outer rims.

These were our hoops and we quickly became proficient in their use. Using a small stick you hit the rim to start it rolling. Then running the stick along the inside of the rim the hoop turned, left rim to turn right and right rim to turn left. This started the first of our racing ideas. Two boys at a time would race their hoops against one another, each ran in opposite directions and the first one back to the starting position was declared the winner. I did this many times but didn't win very often. My legs were too short to run as fast as the others so I was at a disadvantage. But I loved the excitement of these races and was as good as the rest of them at controlling my hoop.

We then moved on and became really adventurous. Not only did the railway line have a rubbish tip, many of the bombsites did as well. We found, in various places, old bicycle frames and wheels in good condition. Again, with help from our fathers, these were made into rideable bikes. We needed help with things like nuts to secure the wheels in the frames, and oil to help them move at speed. We had saddles to sit on, but no tyres, inner tubes, pedals or chains. So propulsion was by boy power. Once we managed to learn the art of balancing a bike unaided, two boys, one on each side, would push, running with all their might until propulsion was achieved. Then we would clatter along the pavement until the bikes ran out of steam and stopped. This was fine for a time but we quickly grew tired of it because they didn't travel very far and we were always being told off about the noise.

So a new track was found, this was at the top of the cut way between Spagagna's and Sangster's. The bikes were pushed down the wide and steep top part where it then became necessary to make a sharp right-hand turn to go down the smaller slope running alongside the back gardens on that side of the road. Eventually they would come to a stop, one boy being stationed down there to mark where each run ended. The boy going the furthest before stopping was declared the winner.

Pat Marriot got this quite spectacularly wrong. Being pushed off by David Simmonds on one side and Bobby Westmore on the other, we all watched as he flew down the first part to reach the turn. It was here that disaster struck. For some reason that not even Pat knew afterwards, he didn't turn but went straight on into the Whelan's back garden, taking part of their fence with him. Mrs Whelan, who did all of the gardening for her family, was outside and saw this terrible apparition coming towards her. Yelling continuously, his arms and legs flying wide, Pat hit a concrete shelf. The momentum of speed and the collision sent his bike flying into the air to effortlessly clear the trench. Crashing through the fence he ended in an undistinguished heap in the middle of Mrs Whelan's runner beans. Pat quickly picked himself up and with a mumbled 'Sorry' ran off. But everyone knew one another, so when he eventually arrived home, he found his own mother knew all about the destruction of the Whelan's garden. In consequence Pat had difficulty sitting down for the next few days.

Inside the house George and I were beginning to find a big difference, starting with shopping, which always took place on a Saturday. We had to accompany mum as she went first to Chandler's, where we were registered for groceries, then to Lowman's for bread and finally Martin's the butcher for our meat – not forgetting to go to the fish mongers for the cat's fish as well. This was mind-blowingly boring. Because we were such a close knit community, mum was well known to all the shop assistants, which meant my brother and I had to endure endless conversations between her and a succession of women standing behind various counters.

Finally mum would produce her little book and the provisions would start to pile up on the counter. In Chandler's it was tins and jars, as well as things that had to be weighed. Sugar was bought by the pound and placed into a homemade bag of blue paper that was rolled into a cone shape then folded over at the bottom. Biscuits were similarly weighed and sold, again by the pound. In our case always the same varieties, 'Marie' or 'Rich Tea'. These were sweet plain biscuits and were displayed in big tins with lids that had a window to see through. Bacon was sliced as required and wrapped in greaseproof paper, each family only being able to buy a certain amount of slices each week.

We would also buy bacon bones for a penny when they were available. These were soaked then boiled to get all the goodness out of them and take any meat still clinging on. Then, once the fat had been strained off, finely diced vegetables were added, the last ingredient being a block of pea soup. Then a delicious bacon bone soup was ready for us to pounce on. Things like this were produced to supplement the harsh budget we were under. I loved that soup and always copied Oliver Twist in asking for more. I also liked vegetables, especially cabbage, which was unusual. Most boys hated it, including my brother George. Mum often got it wrong at meal times, giving me next to no cabbage and George half a plateful. It was no use telling her this was wrong, she simply said, 'No it isn't I know what I'm doing.' We found it easier to simply swap plates to redress the balance.

When mum had finally ordered all she wanted from Chandler's, the produce was packed away into her two shopping bags, while she went up to the till. It was pay for last week and tick up for this as we were always a week behind. The assistant took her money then went to the till but was not allowed to open it, she had to stand there and yell 'cash please.' This brought the manageress out to take the money and dispense the change. This routine was repeated in the bakers where loaves of bread, usually four at a time, were purchased, wrapped in greaseproof paper and put into the bags, which were becoming very full indeed by now. In fact the only trader who was paid each Saturday for the goods he actually sold was the fishmonger, Blitzie the cat's weekly treat of fish heads, fins and tails, bought for 6d.

When the shopping was finally complete the bags had to be carried home. Packed full as they were with not only groceries but vegetables as well, the weight was daunting. She always carried one of these bags herself, leaving George and I to carry the other one between us. Taking a handle each we staggered along the road, often wobbling all over the place, before thankfully reaching home and dumping our burden on the kitchen floor. We were not tall enough to reach up and place the bag on the kitchen table. Then we had to unpack and put away the shopping, helped by Pat and Sue.

Most of the week's provisions went into the sideboard. Only the vegetables were left out, they went out into the scullery. One loaf of bread was taken out of its grease-proof paper wrapping; this was the next one to be used and it was always placed on the breadboard ready for cutting. Children were never allowed to do this because the large bread knife was needed and accidents could happen. Another consideration was that the slices had to be cut as straight as possible and thin. Nobody had sliced bread then, so this was important to make each loaf go around as much as possible.

Because this took all morning to complete, we always had chips, usually with a fried egg, for our dinner. And more often than not it was my job to go to the fish and chip shop to get them. This was Lock's, and as so many other families did the same thing, the queue was right out in the road – which meant a very long wait to get to the counter. I could never see over the top of it, and when it was my turn to be served the assistants didn't know I was there.

Sometimes I was lucky and the grown-up behind lifted me so I could be seen. But more often than not I had to rely on lifting my arm straight up above my head to show them the note from my mother with our order, along with the money to pay for the chips. The order was eventually passed over the top of the counter down to me, along with any change. The only thing I actually liked about the Saturday chip run was that the fat made the newspaper soggy so I could push my finger through and help myself to some of the chips as I went.

Monday was always wash day. Whatever the weather the gas was lit under the copper in the scullery and all our family's washing was pushed inside to be boiled clean. This meant shirts, trousers, dresses, blouses, underwear, as well as towels and other essential household requirements. When the washing cycle was completed to my mother's satisfaction the gas was turned out and, using a stick, the washing was hooked out and put into the kitchen sink for rinsing.

When George and I came home from afternoon school we had the dreaded mangle duty. Although designed as a household help, these devices were sheer murder to operate. The ones most people had then were big wrought-iron monsters, standing at least 5ft high with huge wooden rollers. An enormous handle had to be turned to make these rotate. As the washing was forced through the water was squeezed out of it. A wheel on the top would, when turned down, bring the rollers closer together to give maximum squeezing power. We had to turn the handle as mum pushed the washing through, while Sue and Pat waited to take it out the other side and place it in a bowl to be pegged on the line.

On ordinary days, when we only had the family washing, it was bad enough. With so many things being put through together, George and I had to pull with our combined strength to keep the handle turning, often being pulled right off our feet. Mum would roar at us to 'keep turning' as we fought to comply, always ending up in an exhausted heap on the ground at the end.

This was even worse on sheets week. The task of washing, drying, and ironing took a minimum of two days, providing Monday was not wet. Secondly this was the 1940s and nobody had anything as luxurious as a linen cupboard, with a supply of spare bed linen. While our sheets were being washed we had to make do without. Nights spent in bed with only the very rough blankets we had for covers was no joke at all. Putting those sheets through the mangle was nothing short of slave labour. It was always wonderful when they were eventually dried and ironed and back on our beds. But boy did we have to work hard to achieve this.

The irons were flat, heavy and had to be heated on the gas stove. While one was on, the ironing was being done with the other. When this cooled it was taken out to the scullery and swapped over. The whole iron got hot, including the handle, so it was necessary to use a cloth. The problem here, quite apart from the fact mum had to keep going from one room to another, was there was no heat control. More than once when they were placed onto one of dad's shirts, there was an immediate smell of burning and the shirt would have a black burn mark the same shape as the iron. There was nothing that could be done about it and more than one man ended up wearing shirts with this black imprint on the back.

Clothes, for best wear, were bought for all four of us, once a year, all other ones being hand-me-downs. For boys this meant a suit, shoes and a good winter coat. For the girls it was dresses, shoes and winter coats. For this mum used a cheque from her insurance agent. These could only be redeemed in certain shops and were paid for by weekly amounts. The boy's things were bought in a shop at Portswood Junction called Crosses. The girls had to be taken to a shop in Bevois Valley.

Crosses always fascinated me because it was so huge. When mum was eventually served and handed the cheque to the sales girl it was put into a little brass tube. This was then sealed and the girl pushed a small lever down. Then the tube disappeared along a pulley line that criss-crossed the stores ceiling and wound up in the cash office somewhere upstairs. It would come whizzing back containing mum's receipt and the cheque itself if there was any more credit left on it.

How many times did I watch and fantasise about swinging along those wires myself? I could have found out where they all went, and what a smashing view I would have of the entire shop as I zipped along overhead. Sadly though, this could never happen. For one thing those thin wires would never take the weight, even a skinny little tyke like me. And my mother would have a fit if one of her children behaved in such a disgraceful way in public.

From a very early age good behaviour was drummed into us; when out any-where with our parents we did exactly as we were told. We always stood close to them, never saying a word and certainly never being a nuisance to other people. We always had to be out of the way, never getting under anyone's feet. When on the tram, if it became crowded we were taken out of our seat and had to either sit on mother's lap or stand. This was so that adults, especially ladies, could sit down. Even if it had been possible, zooming across the ceiling of a respectable clothes shop would have broken every rule in the book. We knew the scale of naughtiness and the punishment meted out and acted accordingly.

## 6

# *Slaughter House Grand Prix*

Events were about to catch up with George and I, that would eclipse even the trials of the mangle chore, in a big way. For some time now we had been going regularly to gran's in Mayfield Road. In 1947 mum's younger brother, Ken, got married and was living with his new bride on the top floor of her house. We had never heard of coke but it was cheap and burned well, especially in a kitchen range. Mum was quick to see the potential, so on Saturday morning Uncle Ken turned up at our house. We were glad to see him because whatever he wanted, it would get us out of the dreaded shopping trip.

First of all George and I were told to take the rickety pushchair out of the garden shed then go up to the tram stop. We rode it until reaching the end of St Mary's Street, in the Northam area of Southampton, then followed our uncle to an area known as Chapel where the town's gas works were to be found. This was a large area with an awful smell where coal was burnt and the gas was removed, turning it into husks. There were huge mounds of this and long queues of people just like us who were there to take advantage of this cheap means of fuel.

We went into a little office where uncle paid our 2/- for a hundredweight of coke and was given a little brass tab with a number on. Joining the queue at the loading area we eventually came to the front and gave it to the man. He placed a sack onto the scale underneath the shoot then pulled on a wire to release the coke. When the required weight was reached he lifted the sack off and heaved it into our pushchair. 'Right nippers,' he said, 'off you go, and remember when you come back here again, bring that ruddy sack back.'

Out again on the pavement, Uncle Ken told us we had to get the coke back home. This we saw as no great problem; once the pushchair was on the tram all we had to do was push it round the corner of Belgrave Road. Unfortunately, this was not the case. There was no way any tram driver would take this much weight on – it would be extremely dangerous and nearly impossible to load. This left us with a daunting prospect.; the only way this coke would reach home was for George and I to push it there.

When the full implication of this sank in we were panic stricken. Besides the weight of the pushchair, neither of us knew where we were or had the least idea how to get home. Uncle Ken had thought of that and had drawn us a map. Presenting us with this he pointed in the right direction then turned to get his tram. George and I looked at one another, then at the pushchair standing between us. With a huge shrug of resolution we began to push our load in the direction we had been given. This, if followed correctly, would take us home.

Two little boys really gave it their all to get this enormous weight moving. What we didn't know was that both our sisters had already faced this dilemma but it was just too much for them. It was not something young ladies were expected to do, so the responsibility was handed to us. Our size wasn't even considered, we were boys so therefore strong enough. The wheels of the pushchair were rickety, so getting on and off the pavements was a minor miracle.

Our route took us from Chapel to Mount Pleasant Road and the level crossing over the railway line. When the gates were closed we had to wait for the train to pass before we could go across. This proved to be an ordeal, especially the first time we tried it. Even though the railway lines were sunk into the ground, there were still a lot of bumps and our pushchair wobbled alarmingly. But with a super human effort we made it and went round the corner and down Empress Road. This was where mum had spent most of her youth, living with great-grandmother, and it was where she met dad. But we didn't have time to dwell on this, because waiting just around the corner was another near impossible obstacle.

We needed to go back across the railway then take a sharp right-turn into Priory Road. When we reached the road bridge the dismay we both felt was total. One side was uphill, then after rounding the top flat part we would come back down. Both would prove to be hazardous. With a dragging resolution we started up the first part, but it just got steeper and the load heavier as a result. We began to labour, our breath coming out in whoops. 'Push harder,' George yelled at me. 'I am, I am', I bellowed, to which George replied, 'No you're not. Push harder or we won't make it.'

I pushed with everything I had and my brother did the same. Somehow we made it to the top and took a well deserved rest before starting what we thought would be the easy part. Not a bit of it; the pushchair gained momentum on the downward slope then speeded up alarmingly. George and I realised this and tried desperately to control it. Now he was yelling at me to hold it back but I was simply being pulled along as we ran amok before thankfully coming to a stop at the far pavement of Priory Road.

After following it down and crossing the very busy St Denys' Road, we reached the black arched railway bridge at Kent Road. This was the scene of many a trapped lorry over the years where drivers underestimated the height and became stuck. Finally reaching our house, we now had to get the sack out of the pushchair into the back garden, a task that was quite literally beyond the combined strength of my brother and me. Fortunately it was Saturday and men were at home, so one of them came across and effortlessly lifted the full sack out of the pushchair before carrying it through the house and out into the garden shed. A long hard struggle had reached a successful conclusion, though neither of us could have told you how we did it.

That coke did burn bright red in the kitchen range and was marvellous for using our dad's homemade toasting fork, a long piece of wire with two prongs at the end with which we pierced the bread mum cut for us. Thicker than normal, we had the most wonderful brown toasted bread spread with either margarine or beef dripping. Also Lock's fish and chip shop had started opening for one evening a week. On Friday, we could sit by this coke fire after our regular baths and eat toast with chips, washed down with cocoa.

The coke run went on for many weeks, with one disaster after another happening on the way home. More than once, one of the wheels of the pushchair came off and we had to wait for a grown-up to come along and help us. We would ask if they had any matches. One of these was then broken in half and pushed through the hole at the end of the axel to stop the wheel from coming off again. Inevitably, one day the sack gave an alarming lurch and, before our horrified eyes, it slid out of the pushchair. This was memorable because it happened as we were crossing the railway line at Mount Pleasant with a train due at any moment.

'Get that sack off the track, there's a bleeding train coming,' the signalman shouted at us, as he leaned out the window. We would have loved nothing better but it weighed a hundredweight and we simply couldn't lift it. We heaved and pulled but had no success at all. With a train about to thunder by and sweep our precious coke along with it, our minds turned to the fate awaiting us at home if we returned empty handed. Despite our obvious efforts we were being continually shouted at by the agitated signalman who wanted to close the gates.

Fortunately our predicament had been spotted by a man who came running to help. Telling us to get the pushchair off the track, he picked up the coke and carried it clear of the crossing. The gates were closed and in just a few minutes an express train flew past over that very spot. It was with great relief that George and I thanked the man who helped us and even placed the coke back in the pushchair. Eventually dad gave up the sea and got another job driving a lorry. So he took over this duty.

Now we were free to take advantage of an exciting new venture that was to happen every Saturday morning. This was in March 1948 and the event was the ABC Minors. We had discovered the joys of the cinema and where they were to be found. In our area there were three. The Savoy in Swaythling was affectionately known as the 'cabbage'. The other two were in Portswood, the Palladium and the Broadway, which was the largest. We seldom went in there, but were always to be found at either of the other two.

Not only were these small and cosy, they showed a large selection of films every week. With television still very much in the future, this was the only way to watch them. When both films carried U certificates, or two Us, we could get in with no trouble. But if one of them was an A, and needed to be accompanied by an adult, then we needed help. Since we never went with our parents we would wait outside until a suitable looking adult came along. Then speaking in our best tones of politeness we would ask if they would be good enough to take us in with them.

This usually worked because the adults knew we were merely asking them to get us into the cinema, past the ticket office and into the auditorium. Once inside we would pair off and get to our usual front row seats. And of course we paid for our own ticket which was then 9*d* for children. There were newsreels under the heading of Pathe News, and in this way we kept up with the many things happening in the world around us.

None of this really bothered me at all, but one film certainly did. This was *Snow White and the seven Dwarves,* and I still remember the fright I got at the transformation scene. Witches were one of the things that frightened all of us and I spent a terrifying night with my mother having to stay close at all times. I was convinced the witch from the film was outside on her broomstick and if I was left alone she would fly into the bedroom and carry me off.

When news got out that the Minors would be held at the Broadway we were terribly excited. This was for children only and the entry price was just 6*d.* What a time that was when I turned up along with Sue, Pat and George. This cinema was huge with three floors of seats, and could accommodate a great many people. As we approached on that first Saturday, it was to find a queue stretching as far as the car park right around the back. And everyone here was a child of not more than eleven years of age.

Surprisingly this moved quickly and in no time at all we found ourselves inside the foyer. Going up to pay our 6*d* entrance fee, we were given a membership card and a badge with ABC Minor on it in red. The noise level from two or three thousand children was deafening. I had no idea there were so many kids in this town but every district had brought their children. We were sitting in the top balcony and had a good view as the Broadway's manager appeared on the stage in front of the big screen and was introduced to us as Uncle John. When enough order was gained he welcomed us officially to the Minors and said he hoped to see us there every week from now on. 'We will all now sing the Minors song,' he shouted; the weekly traditional singing began there on that first day.

The words were displayed on the screen but I'm really not so sure about one of the lines. We were supposed to all be 'pals together' but when that many children are assembled under one roof there is bound to be trouble. From that first morning, and for many more after that, the Minors became a battle ground. We would go armed with elastic bands and anything that could be used as a pellet to fire at the other kids. Sometimes this was rolled up paper or small stones, and occasionally, whenever we could get them, dried peas. Missiles were constantly flying through the air as the films were being shown. No real offence was taken at being hit, instead just a determination to get the offender back as soon as possible.

The films were ancient westerns from the thirties. None of us were even born when they were made. There was also a serial that ended with the hero hurtling to his death, either trapped in a car that went over a cliff, or in a building that blew up. Every time when next week's episode was shown he managed to escape just in time. It was blatant cheating but we loved it.

Every week there was a parade of boys and girls whose birthdays had fallen in the week before the Saturday Minors or actually on the day. Didn't I love it when in December 1948 I went up to stand at the side of Uncle John, now as an eight year old. With the card given to me by the Broadway staff clutched tightly in my hand, I listened to the ear-splitting sound of so many voices singing the birthday song and have never forgotten the thrill of that occasion.

Comic swapping was set up soon after the start of the Minors and kept up over a long period of time. This took place outside the cinema after the show, where hordes of kids mingled with each other. Everyone was holding their collection of American comics. We were privileged to have four: the *Dandy*, the *Beano,* the *Eagle* and the *Topper*. Most households had these every week from their newsagents so there was no need for us to swap as we had all read them.

The American comics were a different proposition altogether. We had been able to get these for just over a year and they could be purchased at newsagents for the huge price of 6*d*. We had a selection of *Superman, Batman, Spiderman and Wonder Woman*, as well as, Disney characters like Mickie Mouse, Bugs Bunny, Donald Duck and Porky Pig. But at this price they were not easy to come by and had to be worked for. Once you had a collection you could always swap with other children. The Minors was the best place to do this and with so many titles on view you could always find new comics to read every week.

The fair was now re-established on the common each Easter, Whitson and August Bank Holiday. It was even more exciting this year because dad was home. He sent us off under Sue's care with a whole pound between us. This was a fortune; you could ransom a prince with money like that and dad had given it to Sue to share among the four of us. This meant we had 5/- each and it was the most I had ever had all to myself. I had the time of my life, enjoying the rides and winning prizes at the stalls, spending money with gay abandon. We always went home laden down with the prizes we had won.

Even when the fair was gone, the Common played a large part in our grow-ing up. This is a large open stretch of grassland with criss-crossing paths around some beautiful and picturesque lakes. Put there for the people of Southampton to enjoy, it has always been a favourite place for children to play and dog owners to exercise their pets. At least four of these lakes had wildlife that we loved to watch, particularly in the spring when new ducklings and swan cygnets arrived. But most important for us was the kiddies' paddling pool. Here our entire contingent learned to swim in the one place where the water was deep enough. Most of the time it barely covered our ankles, but over the drain the water was at least 3ft deep.

By this time we had been taken by the school to one of Southampton's swim-ming pools. The outside one was known as the Lido and was only open in the summer months. The other was indoors and reached by walking down one of the steepest roads I ever had to negotiate. People lived here, and how they kept their balance was a mystery to me. Directly at the bottom was the swimming baths.

There were instructors, but most of us, and this certainly included me, found learning to swim here impossible. Victorian is the only word that can be used to describe this place. The building itself was old and gloomy and the pool was sunken with changing rooms around the sides. At its deepest end it was 6ft, and at the shal-low end it was a mere 2ft. I didn't like the place and so I could never relax. All the instructors did was shout at us, 'Get in the water, get under the water, and use your arms and legs. What the blazes do you think you've got them for?'

There was none of today's gentle approach to help with the trauma of first putting your head under the surface. Rubber mats were thrown into the pool and we were told to, 'Get under the water and get those dammed mats back.' All this achieved was to frighten and put us off at the same time. Consequently I made no progress.

But the paddling pool was quite different. We all plucked up courage, egging each other on to take that one deep breath, and dive under the surface. I got used to doing it and finally experienced the magic of opening my eyes under water. I could see the drain much closer now and the bottom of the pool. And by using my arms and legs I began to move about and was actually swimming. Only under the water though, I was no good at all on the surface. But now we could get by, and over the next few years found other places to swim, especially the River Itchen.

Swimming in those days caused some embarrassment due to the bathing cos-tumes we wore. They were one piece, over the shoulder style and all homemade, or, to be more accurate, home knitted. Yes, they were woollen and when dry fitted us comfortably. But emerging from the water in soaking wet bathers, we realised how much wool holds water. They used to droop so much with the weight that the crotch hung down around our knees.

A new era in public transport opened in 1948 with the passing of the trams and the introduction of the bus service in Southampton. The last tram travelled through the town decorated with lights, streamers and balloons, going for the last time under the Bargate Arch. Buses did not use the arch but went around it. This nearly ended in disaster for me. For all my life so far I had travelled on the trams with my mother. The routine had always been the same and because they travelled on rails we had to walk out into the road in order to board.

As far as I was concerned nothing had changed, except for the fact we were now going to get on a bus instead of a tram. So when I heard someone say, 'Here's the bus' and saw it coming, I automatically walked off the pavement into the road only to find the bus had changed direction and was now headed directly towards me. The driver sounded his horn, which nearly deafened me, and I froze with fear. I would have been hit and probably killed had it not been for the bravery of a man in the bus queue. He leaped into the road straight in front of the moving bus and snatched me to safety. Who this man was I have never known, but I know I owe him a great debt.

In April 1948 my idyllic life really declined, and I had to come to terms with that all-time catastrophe experienced by young children everywhere. Having been able to get away with anything by virtue of being the youngest, I acquired that scene-stealing bundle of trouble, called a younger brother. It all seemed so innocent at first.

It was 5 April when Sue, Pat, George and I came running in at the end of afternoon school for our usual tea of bread and plum jam. This was sometimes supplemented with beef dripping. Here we dug the knife as deep into the bowl as we could to scoop up the meat essence that always sank to the bottom. If we were very lucky we had sugar. After spreading a piece of bread with margarine it was then pressed down into the sugar bowl. Today though, we found not our mother but Mrs Biggs waiting for us.

To say this was an astonishing sight is just about the biggest understatement possible. Where was mum? She was always here when we came home so none of us could understand what was happening.

'Mummy has gone away for a few days for a holiday,' said Mrs Biggs, but this didn't put our minds at rest. She had never done anything like this before or been away from home so it was all very confusing. 'Your mother has gone to a holiday camp for a few days, but you won't have anything to worry about because I will be looking after you.'

That part was fine because we were given food we didn't normally see, let alone eat. Of course, where our mother had really gone was to the maternity unit, but it still amazes me that we knew nothing about this at all. We hadn't noticed her getting bigger than usual over the past few months. We were told nothing, so when mum came home we were overjoyed to see her. As the youngest in the family I had missed her more than the others, although I enjoyed the treatment I got from Mrs Biggs, especially the extra treats and cuddles whenever I started to cry for mummy.

Coming into the kitchen just over a week later to find mum there, I rushed into her arms and cried with sheer delight and relief. Without realizing it myself I had started to fear I would never see her again. After the emotional greeting I was disentangled and told I was about to meet my brother. What were they talking about? My brother was standing right next to me. I saw him every day and didn't need to meet him.

With a smile on her face my mother told me she wasn't talking about George. I was led, with the others close behind, over to the sofa. There was a shawl which, when pulled back, revealed a little face. This was my new brother Ron, but where had he come from? Many mothers had given birth to new babies in the road. The discussions that took place about their origins were quite varied.

The most common answer to this question was they were brought by storks, though as none of us had ever seen a stork before it is difficult to see how we clung to this theory. Other suggestions ranged from finding babies in cabbage patches, the baby fairy, and God lowering them down from Heaven. I wanted a straight answer to where this brother of mine had come from. I was astonished when Mrs Biggs took the trouble to explain it all to me in great detail. Now I was over the moon, what power I had to wield in the gang. Not only did I know where babies came from, I had been given this information by a grown-up, so it couldn't be wrong.

As I ran up the road the next day I really felt this was one of those important times in my life. I had never been a prominent member of the Belgrave community because of my small size and natural shyness. Now though I came into my own because I knew something of great importance that none of the others did, and I was going to enjoy it to the full.

As usual there was a gathering outside which consisted of Dave Simmonds, Pat Marriot, Bobbie Westmore, Victor Warrender, John Bates, the Priestly brothers and Edwin Whelan. As soon as I joined them I shouted out, 'I know where babies come from.' This news was received with complete silence at first, which disappointed me somewhat. 'Ok, where then?' asked Pat.

Brushing aside all the things we had previously believed I went carefully into this story. Namely that when my mother went for her holiday she spent some time looking around, and when she came to the baby shop she saw my little brother and decided to bring him home. So that's where babies come from, the shop at the holiday camp.

This news was received with stunned silence but this quickly changed to uproarious laughter. Nobody believed me and I was most upset. I clung to the fact that a grownup had told me so it must be true. Pat kept to his theory that all babies were found in the cabbage patch but, for once, I stood up to him. I was usually very wary around Pat but told him this couldn't be true because we didn't have any cabbages growing in our garden. Dad worked very long hours in order to keep a roof over our heads and didn't have time to tend the garden as well. The only things growing there now were weeds.

This didn't ruffle Pat at all. The fairy bringing the baby delivered it to the cabbage patch nearest your house and then pushed a note through your door to let your mum know it was there. I stamped my foot in frustration at this, clinging tenaciously to the baby-shop theory, even when John Bates pointed out that none of their mother's had been to holiday camps, yet they had new babies – so where had they come from?

This stumped me until Dave Simmonds unexpectedly came to the rescue. 'Maybe they deliver them?'

'See,' I shouted in triumph, 'that's what happens; the holiday camp delivers the babies if your mum can't go there themself.' A mild victory, this was better than nothing. It sufficed for the next year or so until, inevitably, Pat Marriot came up with the real explanation of the mystery of childbirth. Where he got the information from, I never found out. But he had been told that men and woman get together and intercourse takes place between them then the baby is formed inside the mother.

This was a great theory but there was one thing wrong with it: we thought anyone actually doing this was very rude indeed. Now Pat was saying this was how babies are born so my parents must also have done something as unacceptable as this. The idea completely shocked me and I was stung into action. I actually flew at Pat and tried to hit him – a very unwise thing to do and I came out much worse for wear. But I had to make the point and stand up for my mother's reputation.

Edwin Whelan found out about childbirth in his own unique way. Having been punished for some misdemeanour he had been confined to his room and, sitting there waiting to be allowed out, he actually came across a magazine with an article about childbirth. When his mother came up to tell him his punishment was over and he could come back downstairs he asked her what a 'wom' was. This was his pronunciation of the word womb. She was so amused by this that she took the trouble to explain it to him as well as the correct way to say it.

Around this time of year the River Itchen had spring tides, and then we discovered why there were no houses built on the bombed buildings. It was because the water from the river overflowed and spread across to the railway bank. It then came straight on through and flooded not only the bombed buildings but a large part of the road. While this was always a complete nuisance to the residents it was an absolute joy for us as we had our own fairly deep paddling pool. We always made full use of it, splashing and falling about in the water, getting not only very wet but extremely muddy as well. We didn't mind at all but our mothers were not anywhere near as enthusiastic. We were told that 'money doesn't grow on trees' and 'clothes don't come free, they have to be bought.' This was not strictly true because the clothes we wore to play in were all hand-me-downs.

This was why we always had to decide, when one catastrophe after another resulted in torn and dirty clothing, exactly what we would tell them when we got home. As this happened on so many occasions we formed the 'what shall we tell mum' club. Careful explanations were needed which were thoroughly rehearsed before we reached home.

We would be playing in one of the many bombed-out buildings in the area when either Pat or John Bates would suggest some hair brained and impossible task for us to do. The trouble with this is they would always do it themselves, making it imperative for the rest of us to follow suit. On one of these occasions we had been playing in a particularly badly ruined house which still had the staircase, including the banister. Now we weren't allowed to slide down these at home, so to find a ruin with one of these intact was a great discovery and we enjoyed ourselves enormously. Taking it in turns to slide down from top to bottom, Pat then suggested we should try sliding down together.

All of us got astride the banister. Then when the word 'go' was shouted we would slide down in one long chain to finish up in a tangled heap on the floor, out of breath but all laughing and enjoying it immensely. That is until we tried it once too often. As we were sliding down we heard a most alarming groaning sound, then the banister came away from the wall and crashed down. The impact of several boys, plus the weight of the banister, was too much for the already weakened floor to take. So that too collapsed and we all went through into what had once been the cellar.

Amazingly no-one was hurt, but when we examined ourselves not one of us was intact clothes-wise. There were torn shirts, ripped trousers, scuffed shoes, and a great assortment of scratches and bruises. We all looked in gloom, first at ourselves, then at each other and the same thought was in all of our minds. What are we going to tell mum?

This was when the serious discussions took place. We could say a lorry ran onto the pavement and we had to dive into a bush to avoid being hurt. Or the bridge we were standing on collapsed. Some of the ideas put forward were ingenious but unfortunately impossible. So we were rarely believed and always got slapped around the arms and legs as the first part of the punishment.

The second part was when our mothers set to work to mend our clothes and make them wearable again. This meant we would be walking around in stitched up shirts and wearing trousers that had patches over the holes. I don't know how the others felt about this but I personally would have settled for the holes, rather than have to go around with a patch over the seat of my pants. Sometimes this wasn't even the same colour material. My mother was really annoyed when I tore the seat right out of a pair of school trousers. These were grey flannel, and to teach me a lesson and try to make me more responsible in the future she patched them with a piece of bright blue material.

I still shudder as I remember walking into the playground of Portswood Juniors the next day. My friends were unmerciful and made my life hell for the rest of that week, until, mum thankfully relented, and obtained a new pair (well hand-me-downs from one of the neighbours), for me to wear to school. This should have taught me to be more careful, but it didn't. I continued to tear my clothes as well as falling or jumping into water.

Things were very different at home since the arrival of my new brother. Ronald Marsh was now nearly three months old and was lying on the sofa with his feed bottle propped up on a pillow so that he could drink from it. I had been told to watch him as his bottle might slip. But this is not the most exciting thing in the world for an eight-year-old boy to be doing and I very quickly lost interest and started to clown around with George.

When mum came back into the room the bottle had fallen, not only off the pillow but onto the floor. I felt a very hard slap landing on the back of my leg and yelped with pain

'Your brother's bottle has fallen on the floor, I told you to watch him,' mum shouted at me.

'It wasn't my fault,' I said 'I didn't drop it.'

Then the dreaded words I had heard her use so many times to the others fell on my ears instead, 'You're older than him you should have been watching.'

Retribution had arrived with a vengeance. I know of course I should have been able to accept this in good grace; after all I had enjoyed eight years of getting away with it. But I am ashamed to say I felt only resentment towards my innocent younger brother. As the years went on he had to become very wary indeed whenever I was around. I never missed the chance to give him a clip round the ear. I felt he had destroyed my wonderful world. I now know I have good reason to be grateful to Ron because I hate to think what kind of a person I might have become if I had been allowed to keep on getting my own way.

As we were still under rationing and money was tight, many people turned to the practice of keeping chickens. These supplied eggs all year round, and many of the birds themselves ended up on the dinner table at Christmas. The farm lorry came round once a month with newborn chicks and they were for sale at 6d each. I know from personal experience that both Pat Marriot and John Bates had chickens in their gardens because we were constantly roped in for the job of cleaning their runs. It was no fun at all; we had to get right inside and scrape the perches clean using small knives. It was back-breaking work and extremely boring but we did get 6d each for doing it, so it was worth it in the end.

There was also the orange-box lorry. The first time it arrived in Belgrave Road no one could believe what was happening. It was loaded high and when it stopped the men shouted out, 'Anyone want these boxes?' Wood was difficult to come by and now we were being offered it for free

'Yes,' we all yelled and with that the men started to throw them into the road.

This was used for firewood, as well as for mending and replacing fences, sheds and broken door panels. In those days there was hardly a house in Belgrave Road that didn't have at least a fence made from these. Time and again, usually when we were at the table eating our midday meal, the cry of 'orange boxes' would go up outside. This was the only time we were allowed to leave the table without permission. At all other times, once we had finished eating it was necessary to say, 'I've finished can I get down please?' But when the orange boxes arrived we dashed out to get as many of them as we could for our family's use.

Edwin Whelan and I collected enough to build a shed in his back garden and I have always been proud of the way we did this. We knew nothing about building but with advice from our dads we actually managed to build a good sized one. They had to help us with putting up the frame, driving it into the ground so it wouldn't move or collapse when the weather got really bad. Edwin and I spent many days nailing boards onto the sides, front, back and roof. When we finished it looked just as good as any conventional shed and stood in the Whelan's garden for the next nineteen years until the road itself was demolished.

My most vivid memory of the orange boxes was the wonderful use we kids put them to. Pat Marriot had been talking for some time about the homemade trolleys he had seen boys in other roads using. He described them in great detail and we began to get excited about the prospect of building some of these for our own use. But to do this we needed a long plank of wood, at least 6ft long and preferably 2ft wide.

It was an impossible thing for us to find, but here our fathers pitched in to help. My dad knew many people who had building yards, and was able to supply George and I with a plank each. We then had to find a shorter piece of wood, this time only 3ft in length and 6ins wide. This was placed across the front of the plank and secured by a bolt – again supplied by dad and driven through a hole drilled by him and fastened with a large nut. This was not tightened because this was where the front wheels of the trolley would be fixed.

A piece of rope was tied to each side. By pulling on this and pushing the front plank with our feet we could steer with ease. And for the driving seat, what else but an orange box, nailed onto the back of the trolley and just big enough for us to sit in. There was now just one thing needed before these trolleys could be brought into operation. The next few days were spent out and about on the great wheel hunt. We began with the railway line rubbish dump behind our gardens. All the boys scoured this thoroughly and some were successful. But the majority of us had to extend the search further afield, asking relatives if they had any old prams they no longer wanted, and when this produced nothing it was out to the bomb sites again.

Here we met with success in a street of ruined houses. George and I found two old, battered prams that incredibly still had their wheels intact. Carefully we took these off then ran home, full of excitement and clutching our prizes. That evening we delayed our father from getting his usual pint of beer in the Brook Inn because we needed his help to safely fix the wheels, both front and back. There was no sleep that night, knowing that downstairs, just outside the back door were our now finished trolleys.

The next day was the start of six weeks of summer holidays and we joined the rest of the gang, pulling our trolleys behind us. We were super keen to get started and just needed a place where we could race in safety. Both Dave Simmonds and Pat Marriot had already discussed this problem and come up with a solution. The slope opposite gran's house on Mayfield Road, that led down around a sharp bend, then on past the slaughter house, made an ideal race circuit. Once put to us it was agreed with a unanimous verdict.

So on that morning, in bright sunshine, the 1948 Formula 1 Slaughter House Grand Prix season got underway. We took it in turns to be pushers before it was our turn to actually race. This meant two boys to each trolley who waited for the word of command to start. A rag held by one of the girls was brought down sharply then the pushing boys ran from the bottom of Mayfield Road, avoiding any traffic that might be about. This was to get up as much speed as possible before letting go at the top of the slaughter house slope. It was then up to the respective drivers to get their trolley into the best position to win the race.

This meant getting to the bend first. If you could do this you had a definite advantage over the other trolleys, which would either have to go around taking the wide route, which seldom worked, or simply fall behind. Once past the bend it was sit tight, bending forward to cut down wind resistance, and make sure you were first over the winning line. This was marked out by one of the boys or girls standing at the end of the flat straight, at the far side of the slaughter house itself.

When it was my turn to try out my new trolley I was filled with insatiable excitement. As I sat with my pushers waiting for the off, my heart was pounding against my ribs. When the rag dropped I flew across the road, the breath of my pushers in my ears, and then was suddenly free in amongst a dozen others hurtling towards the bend of the slope. I had no chance of winning because I was boxed in towards the centre with no way of gaining a place on the inside to take advantage of the bend. I just had to go with the rest then try to gain a few places on the straight.

Here I was unsuccessful and trailed in right at the back of the field. I put this down to inexperience though George, who had no more than me, had done remarkably better in his two races. Despite this I was determined that next time I raced things would be better. In some respects it was, as I became more skilful at steering and did gain some places to finish higher up the order, but never in the top three. There were regular winners, the most prolific being Dave Simmons. His record of wins was awesome and I started to watch him more than any of the others to see how he did it.

Through this diligent watching I discovered it wasn't just Dave's driving skill, but his trolley that gave him such a huge advantage over the rest of us. He had two very large wheels at the back that gave him much more speed, whereas all of us had smaller ones that were the same size on both front and back. In those days there were two types of pram: the ones with four small wheels, and the other much more expensive versions with two small wheels in front and huge smooth-running ones at the back. It was one of these that Dave had managed to get hold of, so it wasn't any wonder he was the leading driver.

I watched him, repeatedly, with envy, as those great wheels sent him down the slope out in front from start to finish. He didn't win every race he competed in because he, like all the rest of us, had his share of crashes and mishaps. But he was never lower than third place in every race he completed. It therefore became obvious to me that, in order to compete properly with Dave and the rest of the successful drivers, I needed to find an old pram with these large rear wheels. And I was prepared to go to any lengths to get one.

# 7

# Cruising Down the River

Edwin Whelan and I were rapidly becoming best friends. We loved to go near rivers and streams and our favourite pastime was to build dams and see how much water they could hold. After deliberately breaking them, the water surged away like a tidal wave, usually with me standing right in front. This made me wary around water after getting so many hidings for getting my clothes wet.

Two weeks after the big wheel hunt began we were walking beside a wide stream and I saw the very thing I so desperately wanted. Over on the far bank was an old pram with large rear wheels. Quickly forgetting mum's warnings I jumped fully dressed into water which came up to my chest and waded over to the other side. Grabbing the pram, I pulled it into the water then hauled it back to the bank, falling over several times in the process and of course getting fully immersed. But I made it finally and stood next to the laughing Edwin Whelan, yelling with excitement.

The next day, after getting a hiding the night before for the state of my clothes, I began work on the renovation of my racing trolley. With some help from my father, the Jimmy Marsh racing trolley mark two stood proudly ready. I sat in it for the first time while it was still in our back garden and felt such a thrill, because I knew I was going to get much more speed now. The wheels had been carefully oiled, the steering checked, and everything made ready for the next day's racing.

Finally it was Grand Prix number 246, of the 1948 season, and I was on the grid at the bottom of Mayfield Road ready to roll. I had the two best pushers in the business, John Bates and Victor Warrender, ready to give me the start I badly wanted. Again it was my dream girl Vickie Masterman holding the starting flag, and as she brought it down I shouted 'Go'. John and Victor did their part superbly and pushed me into third place at the top of the slope. I could feel the trolley accelerating beneath me and I moved up to second.

Now I had as good a chance as ever of getting to the bend first and actually winning a slaughter house race. There was only one thing wrong; the trolley in front was Dave Simmonds. He had the same size wheels and had been in this position many times before. I was gaining, but not fast enough to take the bend away from him. So I did the only thing I could do under the circumstances and tucked right in behind, intending to try a passing manoeuvre as we flew past the doors of the slaughter house.

Consequently, as we came to the bend I almost hit the back as we locked together on course. It was then things went horribly wrong. Dave's front wheel came off and he crashed in spectacular fashion right in front of me. His trolley broke into pieces and he was thrown clear. Being so close behind I had absolutely no chance of avoiding the wreckage. I hit it squarely, my trolley going over the top of the broken wood, with the result that I actually flew up into the air.

I clung on desperately and turned full circle in the air before going sideways into the slaughter-house wall. I was thrown so hard that the breath was knocked out of my body, but as I lay on the ground there was only one thing on my mind, was my precious trolley alright? As soon as I could stand, I gave it a once-over and was relieved to find that apart from broken wood, which could easily be replaced, the all important wheels I had suffered so much to obtain were alright.

This was more than I could say for myself. I had cuts and scrapes all over my arms and legs, and my clothes were torn to pieces. Poor Dave had suffered too, his trolley was a total write off. For both of us it was back to that all important question of, what shall we tell our mums? I strolled over to see if he was alright and to discuss this bad situation but Phil Scoulart was pointing towards the slaughter house and shouting 'Bull!'

I wasn't very pleased. We had seen bulls being led to the slaughter before and I had much more to worry about now than going over to watch this. But Phil was running towards us, still shouting and pointing back. Everyone who had walked back from the finishing line was standing in a group by the bend in the track. We suddenly paid attention because of the urgency in his voice and saw that there was indeed a bull, not where it was supposed to be; it had escaped and was out in the road unattended.

As the full horror hit us we realised the danger we were in. That bull was mad and we were right in its line of vision. Totally ignoring the slaughter-house staff that had come out to try and recapture this runaway, it put its head down and after pawing the ground began to charge towards us. Pat Marriot's shout galvanized us into action and we ran towards the placards in the grounds of Woodmill Laundry. Not normally a fast climber, fear lent me wings and I got to the top just as fast as everyone else.

We clung on for dear life as the bull hit the bottom of this structure nearly knocking us off. It then began to prowl angrily around and there was no way any of us were going to attempt to come down. Fortunately the slaughter-house men, along with the police, quickly arrived and managed to drive it away, up to Portwsood Road before turning the corner into Belgrave Road. It ran the length of this before being trapped and recaptured on railway property at the back of No.4, the home of the Ford family. I lovingly repaired my trolley and just two weeks later felt light with excitement as I won my first ever Slaughter House Grand Prix.

It was 1949 and the summer holidays were once again beckoning. We still played around the railway and had started going on the line but took adequate precautions. There was no live rail in those days of steam but the risk of being hit by a train was always present. We could see a long way in both directions and always knew when trains were coming, so we never went on if one was in sight. Even Pat Marriot stuck to this rule.

As well as the sewage works there was a lot of ground on the other side of the track. This was flanked by a belt of trees. We found a path leading through the undergrowth and followed this until we came to a small stream with a fallen tree across it. We scrambled over this, thoroughly enjoying ourselves now, and found, to our utter delight, the perfect place for swimming. It had led us directly onto the bank of the River Itchen and just along from where we were standing was a little cove. This was surrounded by trees and there were fallen trunks that made perfect seats.

We found a natural shelf just a few feet down onto which we could climb, from there going straight into the water. None of us needed any persuasion and we stripped down to the bare essentials. Needless to say we used that wonderful place for many years to come and did what boys all over the country loved to do. A rope was fixed to one of the trees and we had the most enormous fun swinging out then letting go and dropping straight into the water, where I became the same as everyone else and swam underwater with ease. The bank was overgrown in places with large lily plants and other weeds, so we imagined it was a jungle and played Tarzan games.

On the bomb site between Brickfield Road and the school in Somerset Road, a dirt track had been set out. This was the home of the newly formed Hawks Cycle Speedway team and gave us our first real hero, apart from the cowboys we idolised on the cinema screen. The Hawks star rider was smaller than most of his team mates but there was very little he couldn't do with a speedway bike. Every time he lined up to take part in a race, we cheered ourselves hoarse as he charged around the track, swinging into the curves with one foot on the ground and pedalling towards the front time and time again. His name was Dan Higgs and he lived with his parents in nearby Northcote Road. The Hawks were a very good team indeed except for one rider who managed to crash every time, and this amused us so much we nicknamed him 'the bike buster'.

Before we knew what was happening it was time to go back to school. This wasn't as bad as previous years because of a new teacher we came to like and respect very much, Mr Hammond; he made every lesson a joy. One of the things he taught us was how radio works, by building our own little studio outside the door with microphones so we could broadcast to our friends inside. I had been sent out with Edwin Whelan to think up and perform a play, using one of four themes we had been provided with. After careful consideration we decided to do the pirate one and began to ad lib this into the microphone.

The problem was we didn't realise we had to stay very close to the microphone in order for our broadcast to be heard. We were running about the hall acting our socks off and getting well out of range. So when we went back into the classroom everyone asked, 'What the blazes was that? We couldn't hear a word.' At least we tried; most homes had a radio so to be doing this was the equivalent of today's children appearing on television.

There was also a horrendous experience waiting for us at Portswood Junior School when we met the infamous 'Dr Drop 'Em'. This was without doubt the most difficult thing I had experienced in my young life so far, coming from such a strict Victorian home. The day the new doctor arrived, a polish woman, we were not alarmed about seeing her for a full medical examination. As usual on these occasions our mothers would be present as we were still just under ten years old.

I was halfway down the line and saw several boys go in before me. They seemed to be most upset when they came out but I didn't know why. When my turn came I stood in front of the doctor, with my mother behind me, when she looked at me.

'Right boy, drop your trousers.' I was hit by shock, what did she say? Surely not what I thought it was. I spun round and looked in horror at mum. She would soon put this right, after all wasn't it she who was always telling me I must never do anything like this in public?

But the appeal in my eyes was wasted. Another aspect of mum's Victorian upbringing was the belief that whatever was said the doctor was always right. So all I got from her was, 'Well you heard what the doctor said, now get on with it.' So, I undid my snake belt and let my trousers drop to the floor. To make matters worse it was in front of a woman, and one who until that moment I had never met. Only my mother and the members of the Belgrave gang had seen me in this position before and my face flamed scarlet red.

She told me to cough, which I did with difficulty. I had to stand while this lady performed the whole medical examination. All the while she was talking to my mother as if I wasn't there. Not until she finished was I allowed to pull my trousers back up. She was telling mum I needed building up with malt and cod liver oil every day. Was there no end to the punishment this terrible woman was inflicting on me?

I knew I was skinny and it didn't bother me at all. I was able to squeeze through the smallest openings and find wonderful places to hide in. I could climb trees with a swiftness that left some of my friends gasping in my wake, and now I could run. Why on earth did I need to be built up? We all have memories from childhood we would rather forget, and taking that medicine was mine. From that day onwards I had to line up and have a large spoonful of the vilest tasting cod-liver oil poured into my mouth, almost making me gag. This was followed, using the same spoon, with equally disgusting malt. And there was nothing I could do to avoid this daily torture.

The malt was doled out every day to those children whose names were on the list; and thanks to 'Dr Drop 'Em' my name was there. In subsequent years, when I have met ex male-pupils, from Portswood School the subject of this doctor always comes up. The routine was the same regardless of our reason for going to see her.

She would glare at me with the same response, 'Right boy drop your trousers.' If I said this wasn't necessary for such a small injury she would roar, 'Are you deaf boy? Didn't you hear what I said? Drop your trousers.' Then of course I would have to comply and was told to cough. Only after this did she get round to asking your reason for visiting. With tears, mostly of embarrassment, streaming down my cheeks I would sob out. 'Please Miss, I've cut my finger. Can I have a plaster?' This happened to every boy in the school at one time or another.

But the academic year went on and we were being prepared for the biggest exam we would take during our school life. This was the scholarship known as the Eleven Plus, to be taken in the summer of 1952, and we were nervous about it. If we passed we would be going to a grammar school for our senior years and I didn't particularly want to do this. Neither did I want to fail, so like the rest I studied, but during that year we found other things more interesting than studying for exams.

I had gone with the others to see a film at the Broadway cinema. We were ABC Minors no longer, and we seldom went there, preferring the Savoy or Palladium. The Savoy was my favourite because we had found a way of getting in for nothing. We were still small enough to get through the window of the gents toilet and from there we sneaked into the auditorium. But there was no way this could be achieved at the Broadway. To reach the stalls in this cinema it was necessary to walk down a stairway before coming to the door at the bottom that led inside.

While we were leaving and walking back up the stairs together, a boy my own age was coming the other way. We politely moved over to give him room to pass, but on seeing me he immediately said ,'Hello Jimmy, how are you?' I had never seen this boy before and had no idea who he was.

'Who are you?' I asked, to which he replied, 'Don't you know me? I'm your cousin.'

He explained that his mother was my father's sister and that made us cousins. Now I knew nothing at all about dad's family apart from Aunty Francis who visited us quite a lot with her husband Jack. They lived at Fair Oak, just outside Southampton and always came on a motorbike. They had one daughter named Jennifer. Of dad's other relations we knew absolutely nothing. So on arriving home I asked my mother about this unknown cousin. She told me dad's sister, Chris, lived in Thackery Road just behind Aunty Ada's house and there was more than one cousin living there.

This was all the information I ever gleaned about my father's family, except that his parents both died before I was born. His mother had lived just long enough to see George born, and had died, content in knowing the Marsh name would be carried on. Why there was so much mystery about his side of the family I have never known but his past was certainly shrouded in it.

Belgrave Road was due to be resurfaced and a fleet of lorries soon turned up to do the tarring and relaying. On one of these the driver had fixed a soft toy, namely my favourite cartoon character Bugs Bunny, to the radiator grill. As we were laughing and admiring this, the driver got out and beckoned George and I to get up into the cab and enjoy a ride – a wonderful opportunity and one we would love to have taken up. But warnings about taking rides from strangers had been driven in very hard over the years, so we politely refused.

The driver was extremely reluctant to take no for an answer and insisted that we get up. My brother and I were now thoroughly alarmed and decided the best thing would be to run home. We didn't have far to go because work had progressed to within a few yards of our home. So we ran as fast as we could and were just blurting out to our mother about the man in the lorry, when we saw he had followed us into our house and was walking through the hall towards us.

We froze with fright and clung to mum. 'Good God Edie, you've trained these two well haven't you,' he said. Mum then introduced us to yet another cousin. Bewilderment turned to delight when we realised this was someone we knew. He was a relation, which meant it was alright for us to ride in his lorry. We were praised for the way we had heeded the warnings about riding with strangers and allowed to spend the rest of the day with our cousin. What a time we had, waving at the rest of the gang who glared in envy as we rode the Bugs Bunny lorry.

At this time I went from being simply a pupil at Sirdar Road Sunday school, to choir boy at South Stoneham Church. This is where Southampton's Halls of Residence are now situated, accommodating hundreds of students who attend Southampton University. Tucked into a corner is the beautiful thirteenth-century church, and here, three times each Sunday, twice in the mornings and evensong in the evening, I dressed in my cassock and sang hymns. I always looked so divine and innocent, which I certainly was not.

We had to put up with choir practice twice a week at the Belgrave Road Hall. This was situated on the side of the bombed buildings and was owned by the church. For singing our hearts out each Sunday we were rewarded with an outing in the summer, usually a trip to the beach, and a party at Christmas. Sunday school was compulsory and something we had to do. Whether this was for our religious education, or just to get rid of us that day I will never know, but even here we made our own fun.

On quite a few occasions we visited Dave Simmonds at his real home opposite South Stoneham cemetery. By doing so we discovered the road bridge over the River Itchen at Mansbridge. It was very narrow, and care had to be taken when playing because of the traffic. There was a large pipe just under the parapet on one side of the bridge that we climbed onto, and from there we leapt straight into the river.

Coming from church one day we were intrigued to see a narrow path leading down into the undergrowth. Being the adventurous crowd we were, we followed this and found, to our great delight, a very-handy shortcut to our new swimming spot. So every Sunday after that, when the weather was good and the evening service was over, the choir boys reverted to type and rushed along the path to the river.

I have to mention the scrap yard that was situated at the top of our road. This was a place of mystery and fright. It was locked at all times and had the most enormous tin gates that rattled and groaned in the wind. It also had a very large snarling black dog. Ordinarily this would have proved irresistible. Pat Marriot would have issued the challenge and one way or another we would have found a way to bypass the dog and get in. Situated between Belgrave Road and our race track and playing field alongside the slaughter house, it would have been a very quick and convenient route for us to take. But not one of us ever entered this yard.

Over the years whenever the old Belgrave gang met up, I posed this question: Why were we so reluctant to go into that metal yard? So far I have not received an answer and it wasn't only us who boycotted it. My father regularly brought home scrap metal, 'spidge' as he called it, which sometimes had plastic coating. He lit a bonfire in the back garden to burn off this unwanted plastic, creating an awful smell in the process. This made all our close neighbours shut their windows in order to keep it out of their homes. It never caused ill feeling, just the cry of, 'Shut your windows, Marshy is burning his spidge again.'

Next day when the metal was ready, dad always took it to St Denys' Metals in Priory Road and sold it to help with the housekeeping. He never took it to the yard at the top, which was a lot closer. For this reason the yard has been a source of mystery and intrigue. The way the gates groaned in the wind gave it a haunted feel. Formerly a knacker's yard where horses were slaughtered, maybe one of them was still there in spirit. This never stopped us playing and racing past the slaughter house though; here we actually watched the animals being killed. There was a yard at the back with a small enclosure surrounded by a 6ft wall. In here the stomach contents of the slaughtered animals were kept, prior to disposal. The skins or stomach linings were used as sausage skins.

Led on by Pat we tried to balance on the outer side of the wall without falling off – easy enough if you were very careful and walked slowly and remembered to lean outward – the idea being, if you did lose your balance you would at least land safely on the grass outside. One by one, we managed it even if we did wobble a lot before reaching the end and jumping safely to the ground.

Then it was Pat's turn and all went well until he was roughly halfway across, where he wobbled and leaned out to correct himself. Thinking he was alright, he leaned the other way to finish the crossing but went too far and we watched in horror as he fell up to his chest in stomach waste. Dragging himself out he tried to join us, but found very quickly that on this day he had absolutely no friends. He was made to walk a long way behind us on the way home, so obnoxious was the smell.

As soon as his mother saw him he was refused entry to the house until he had cleaned the terrible mess off. There was only one way to achieve this. With us trailing gleefully behind, he crossed the railway line to the river and jumped in clothes and all. Staying there until every bit of the muck was gone, he returned home soaking wet and this time was let in, but still suffered a hiding for the state he was in.

In 1950, Mr and Mrs Biggs finally got a place of their own and moved out, leaving the entire house to us for the first time. But a part of them did come back, a large ginger tomcat called Timmy, a kitten of Blitzie, had lived in the front room with the Biggs family. He never adjusted to the new house and ran away back to us where he was allowed to stay. Timmy was a hunter and loved to scavenge along the railway bank after rats and moles. He too ate bread and jam with us all week, then, with Blitz, went crazy at the weekends while he waited for the fish treat to be cooked by my mother. The smell of this was so bad that everyone left the house, but the cats really did love it

Our exploring went on and we found new and exciting places to play. One of these used to be a brick works and was situated just beyond Woodmill, today the site of Bitterne Park Secondary School. The clay pits had a sheer cliff at the top end that tapered right down to almost nothing at the other. It was possible to walk up along a path, starting at the low point and leading right to the top end, but we were never going to take the easy route up. No, we were the Belgrave gang and as such needed a challenge, so we climbed up at the steep end every time. Looking down from here we could see the cliff run straight down until it reached a point where a natural shelf hid the last steep drop to the ground. A picture formed in our minds of a slide with a turn at the bottom, only a few inches away from the edge of this shelf and that last big drop.

We realised that boys before us must have used this slide for fun, and if they could do it then so could we. Looking around we quickly found a number of corrugated tin sheets; these were wet and rusty but usable. Dragging these out into the open, the driest one was soon in position at the top of the slide. One question now remained: who was to have the honour of being the first Belgrave boy to fly down this slope? It was decided after a gang meeting that the short straw method was the fairest way to have our new slide tested. It was one of the Priestly brothers, Brian in this case, who lost.

So he found himself being pushed off by many willing hands before he had time to protest. The tin rushed smoothly down the slope and was rapidly approaching the dreaded drop when Brian leant over to his right clutching the corner. Miraculously, or so it seemed to us, the sheet of tin turned almost 45°, with Brian still clinging on for dear life, and went past the drop. It then rushed on to finish at the bottom some forty yards or so to the right of where it had started its run.

Now of course we all wanted a go and I can still remember the thrill of that turn as the drop rushed towards you, and the effort that was needed to bring your sheet round in time. Also the relief and pleasure as you landed at ground level all in one piece. We spent weeks doing this and in our own way became experts at handling our unorthodox vehicles.

Surrounding the clay pits on all sides were blackberry bushes. We picked for our mothers as well as other relations, as this was one of our means of earning money – it was an ideal place to do it. The fright the clay pit slope gave me had long since turned to joy as I effortlessly did it time and time again. Thrilling to the end. as wind rushed past my face. I got so good that I started to leave the turn to the last possible moment. I began to think of myself as invincible, so it was poetic justice the day Edwin Whelan and I went to the clay pits alone, on a day after it had been raining.

Under these conditions we usually gave this place a miss because the clay would be wet and no good for sliding. However I am always an optimist and tried anyway. Edwin and I reached the top of the slope and I took my place, sitting well forward and hoping for a rush of speed as I took off. Nothing happened despite both our efforts. I grasped the sides of the sheet and bounced forward to try and make it slide, but it stayed stubbornly where it was.

Resignedly I got off and began to accept there would be no runs today when Edwin said, 'Why not try turning it over?' I just looked at him in a stupor; what on earth did he mean? If it wouldn't slide on one side, why on earth would it on the other? The clay was wet, that's why it wouldn't go. But just to humour him I turned the tin over and once more took my place. No sooner had I sat down than it took off. Never had I gone down so fast and I wasn't holding on so the sudden rush of speed knocked me flat on my back.

I struggled into a sitting position, but by this time it was too late to avoid the big drop that was hurtling towards me. I had absolutely no time to lean over to the right and my sheet went straight as a dye. The front end dug into the ground and stopped dead. I did not and, instead, went sailing through the air. Seeing the drop that was now beneath me I carried on flying until I made contact with the ground and had the wind knocked out of my body. I lay in a helpless heap, spread-eagled and unable to move.

Edwin of course was horrified as I lay ominously still. He raced down the path to see if there was anything he could do, only to find me laughing. I have always had the ability to bounce whenever I fall and it certainly came to my rescue here. As I regained my breath I simply continued to laugh, and when Edwin realised that I was quite alright he too joined in.

Just after this incident we discovered the best way to be on the river was by rowing a boat. It was Dave Simmonds who heard about this and we all went to find out. Going to Cobden Bridge, in St Denys' Road, we found a boatyard. A path led us down and we found ourselves for the first time in Dyers. On enquiry we found we could hire rowing boats at a very low hourly rate, the problem being the tiny matter of the deposit.

Mr Dyer was very particular about his boats and always kept them in good repair so they were clean and comfortable to sit in. This was why he demanded a deposit, and it was a whopping 10/-. None of us, no matter how many odd jobs we did, could ever raise this amount of money. So there was only one way it could be achieved and that was to throw ourselves on the mercy of our mothers and ask for a loan.

I vividly remember the reaction when I told mum what I wanted to do. She thought it was a very good idea at first, providing I was careful and didn't do my usual trick of coming home soaking wet with ruined clothing. I hastily assured her on this point then, as casually as I could, mentioned the deposit. 'Oh and how much is that?', she asked. When I told her she stood still before exploding, 'How much? Ten shillings, do you realise that's just about all I've got to last until the end of the week.' I hastily explained it was just a deposit and we got this back when the boats were returned. It took a lot of grovelling and haggling before my mother actually handed me a ten shilling note that I looked at with awe. She was most specific about the fate I would meet if I dared return home without it.

So the adventure began. We had all been successful in borrowing some money and arrived at the boat yard together. Mr Dyer met us on the jetty and proceeded to take our money, then explained the rules to us. One pound ten shillings was taken as deposit for three boats and we were given tickets which we needed to produce in order to get this money back. Also on the ticket was the time we had hired the boats, so that Mr Dyer knew how much to charge us. Then it was down to the water and our first look at the rowing boats that were to give us so much pleasure over the next three years.

My first reaction was one of shock – they were so big and I was so small. But I watched and listened with the others as we were shown how to row and control them. He also gave us a stern warning about not taking the boats out of the water. By this he meant we could row up the river as far as Woodmill and the end of the saltwater-side of the Itchen. But on no account were we to lift the boats out and try to carry them across the road to the fresh water side. We solemnly promised and at last were allowed to get in and row away on our own.

Those boats were wonderful and so well maintained. The seat at the back could accommodate two people with ease. Upholstered in a colourful material it was a luxury to sit on. At the oars was a hard seat with a board by your feet to help with pulling them through the water. The oars themselves were bigger than me and just trying to hold them at first proved nearly impossible. But I do have a very determined streak and started getting the hang of it. At first they went in too deep and I hadn't a hope of pulling them through, or if I pulled too much on one side the boat started going round in circles.

Eventually though we managed to row up the river. We saw many familiar landmarks and when we passed our new swimming spot we stopped and went ashore just for the fun of it. At Woodmill we immediately forgot the promise we had made to Mr Dyer. The boats were pulled out of the water onto the grass. Then one by one all three were across the road and refloated on the fresh water. This had to be done with absolute care because we genuinely didn't want to damage these lovely boats. Not only would this have meant losing our precious deposits, we would have been excluded from ever hiring them again. In all the time we hired Dyers boats not one of us ever lost their deposit.

I am sure Mr Dyer knew we disobeyed him, but overlooked it as the boats were always returned in as good a condition as when we set out. Once on the fresh-water side we were able to row right up under the narrow stone bridge at Mansbridge and further on past the White Swan Inn. This is a lovely public house that backs right on to the river.

One person was always the cause of our downfall, Pat Marriot. He spotted a small tributary branching off to the right. This was overgrown with plants and weeds lying across the surface, but Pat said we should go down to see where it leads. Trying to row through that vegetation was sheer murder and when we came to some overhanging tree branches we lost two overboard. But incredibly we carried on and had a pleasant time admiring the birds and wildlife. Even the two casualties, with their clothes now laid out to dry, joined in. We rowed ourselves out that day and came back exhausted, but very happy, and determined to do it all again.

As summer gave way to autumn we started to gather rubbish for the bonfire on Guy Fawkes Night. We had great fun with bangers once the fireworks appeared in the shops. These were not rationed, and provided we could get the money we could buy as many as we liked. Dave Simmonds came up with the idea of getting empty bottles and weighing these down with stones so they would sink when placed in water.

So it was over the railway line again with our bottles to put Dave's theory to the test. The idea was to place a banger in the bottle, light it and wait for it to fizz, before rapidly putting on the top and pushing it under water. When the banger went off it shattered the bottle and made a wonderful underwater explosion. We had discovered how to make our own depth charges. Many imaginary submarines

were sunk in this way. In fact I believe we won the war single handed. Another use
we found for bangers was to blow up the dams we made over streams. Our bombs
may not have bounced, but watching the water cascading through we were convinced the dam busters of the Second World War had nothing on us.

Bonfire night was held in our back garden, rather than on the bombed buildings
as in previous years. This was because we still had nothing growing and we were
able to utilise the space for the bonfire. The Marriot family, Joe, Dave and Pat came
round bringing fireworks and their guy. My father always supervised these and a
great time was had by all. There were never any accidents because it was carried out
under strict parental guidance.

Around this time mum went to the holiday camp again and stayed for over a
week. Our new neighbour, who had moved into No. 92 with her husband and two
children in place of the Golden family, looked after us. This time the baby shop
had sold out of boys so mum had to buy a girl instead. My youngest sister appeared
in October 1950 and was named Jean. The last one of the family to be born, she
made up an even number of children, although when people commented on this it
somewhat confused me. They said things like, 'You're alright now Mrs Marsh, three
of each.' I didn't understand because although I now had three sisters I only had
two brothers and three and two make five. So how could they say we were an even
family? I never of course included myself in the head count.

My little brother Ron was now a small boy of three and needed very careful
looking after. I really did find out what it had been like for my brother and two
sisters when they tried to keep me under control; and now with a new baby to
contend with as well, life wasn't easy. But I still managed to get out with the gang,
and on one of our trips across the railway line, Bobby Westmore, got his hands on a
real pellet rifle. It was nothing like the cap guns we habitually played with that just
made a loud bang when you pulled the trigger.

This gun actually fired a small lead pellet, which if it hit you could really hurt.
We all had turns at firing this. I was next to useless and hit nothing at all, but Dave
Simmonds was better and so had more turns than the rest of us. But once, when
he aimed the gun up river, hoping to hit a small tree that was partly hidden by
undergrowth, he got a loud yelp of pain instead. Bobby himself came running out
from behind a tree, having gone there to answer a call of nature. The pellet glanced
off the trunk and hit him in the right buttock. Although this must have hurt and of
course was highly embarrassing, it wasn't either of these things that caused Bobby
so much indignation. The situation was made far worse by the fact he had been
shot by his own gun.

We resented any sort of intrusion onto our hallowed playground, the bombed
buildings. This was well established and recognised by everyone in the road. Here
we played cricket using homemade stumps, three pieces of wood driven into the
ground, and football with newspaper stuffed into an old shirt or jumper to make a

ball. A new family had moved into the road. The Brackens had a daughter who was so attractive she knocked the socks off all the boys, including me. Bernice was her name and she used to ride a horse round and round the bombies, our affectionate name for this piece of ground.

With huge indignation we found Tykie McArthur had parked his latest clapped out car, a large London taxi, right in the middle of our ground. He had been buying old bangers for some time now and would drive the length of the road, revving the engines. These always backfired with a loud bang every few yards. While we were happy to watch this spectacle and laugh ourselves silly every time the bangs came, we were much less happy now he had started to park these wrecks on the bombed buildings.

A hurried conference was called and from this a deputation consisting of Dave Simmonds, Bobby Westmore, John Bates and the irrepressible Pat Marriot went up and knocked on Tykie's door. They proceeded to explain the situation, intending to politely ask him to move his vehicle and allow us to get on with our games. What they got from Tykie was a roar and the threat of boxed ears if they didn't immediately remove themselves.

Feeling dejected we got into the taxi – after all it was illegally parked on our ground – to talk over the situation. While we were doing this, John Bates was idly pulling on the overhead upholstery and found a part that was ripped; this quickly became a large tear. Over the next few days, to the fury of Tykie and amusement of everyone else, we reduced that taxi to a shell. This was then used for several weeks as a fort for fighting off hordes of Indians, a pirate ship and a haunted castle. It was eventually towed away for scrap by St Denys' Metals and Tykie never parked there again.

Another threat was audacious and came from outside. Apparently the law, as it stood then, was that if you come across a piece of waste ground and fence it off, you can then claim it as your own, providing the fence stays in place for seven years. When two men arrived and proceeded to fence off our playground, a task that took them all day complete, no one did anything to stop them. But once they had finished and left and our fathers came home from work, we all went down to inspect this addition to the street. Armed with pick axes, sledge hammers and the like, in much less time than it had taken these strangers to put up their fence, it all came tumbling down.

The fence posts and wire netting went into the back gardens of several of the houses in the road. When the men returned a few days later to find their attempt to claim our land had failed, they disappeared, never to be seen again. The irony being if they had been successful they would have inherited a piece of ground they would never have got building permission to use because of the annual flooding.

On Christmas afternoon as the pubs shut, all the grown-ups came out and did a hokey cokey down the centre of the road, led by a remarkable old lady. The Buddon family lived just down the road from us and George and Les, who were both the same age, became very close friends. But it was old Mrs Buddon, their seventy-eight-year-old grandmother who was singing and dancing and leading the line. They went the full length of the road with all of us running alongside. We may not have had much but we really did know how to enjoy ourselves.

As spring approached Ron was coming up to four years old and had learned to avoid me as much as possible. Jean was six months and announcing herself at every opportunity. I was called on more and more to look after them both, a job I disliked very much. Dad decided some things had needed doing for a very long time. There was the matter of a lock on the toilet door, a light on the stairs, and other small jobs. He said it was about time the garden was planted. This was fine except for the fact George and I were roped in to help with the digging. It was back breaking work and we hated it, but when it was done dad spent a lot of time planting lettuce, radishes, carrots, and potatoes. And what a joy it was when these grew to maturity and we were able to enjoy vegetables from our own garden.

Coming home from school I was told a parcel had come and it was placed by the side of my plate at the tea table. Never in my short life had anything come in the post for me. I sent for this with my parent's permission, some six weeks before from a coupon that was in the Dandy comic. I tore the wrapping off to reveal the object of my desire, a torch with batteries. As the evenings were now dark and I wasn't allowed to take it up to the bedroom, I had to wait for the next day when I could try my new treasure out.

The only problem now was that in daylight, torches do not work at their best. But it was Saturday and we always went to gran's, so I ran all the way up Mayfield Road. Then bursting in on her through the side door, I asked if I could play in her coalhouse. I'm sure she thought I had gone mad. 'You can't play in there dear, you'll get filthy and then what will your mother say to me? Anyway why on earth do you want to?'

Proudly I showed her my torch and told gran that her coalhouse, which was a little room just outside the back door opposite the toilet, was the only place I could think of that was dark. So with some misgivings she gave in and for a long time I sat on her coal pile and shone my torch round and round.

Gran Nicholson had bought one of the revolutionary new mangles, a much smaller model with a more efficient handle that turned on ball bearings and was easier to use. Also these were fixed to the side of the kitchen sink, making the job of mangling the clothes much more satisfactory. A few days later disaster struck when mum's mangle broke. This was bad enough in itself, but the remedy was even worse. She needed a replacement and quickly.

Consequently George and I were sent to gran's to ask if she still had her old one and if mum could have it. The answer was yes on both counts and gran was only too pleased to get rid of it. We somehow managed to get the mangle around the side of the house, down the sloping front path and out onto the pavement. So far so good, now all we had to do was get it down Mayfield Road, along Portswood Road and round into Belgrave.

As we started however we found ourselves on a very steep slope. We had walked up many times before and never thought anything of it. Now though we were trying to hold a heavy mangle, and it was just like the coke episode a few years before. One of us was in front and the other behind, but it began to gather speed alarmingly. We shouted desperately to each other to hold on, but it was no use.

The mangle broke free and started careering down towards the main road at the bottom, with George and I in hot pursuit. My mind was racing ahead contemplating the possible scenarios. After reaching the clinic, this road turned to the right. If the mangle went round this turn and stayed on the pavement it would be heading straight for the business premises of Oddie Fasteners, a large building to the right of the slaughter house slope and this would be a disaster. But if it went off the pavement and ran on down the centre of the road all we would have to worry about would be any traffic unlucky enough to arrive at that precise moment. The mangle would run on down the slope, just as we still did on our trolleys, and eventually stop on the straight run past the slaughter house itself.

It stayed on the pavement and reached the end, charged across the main road mercifully hitting nothing, and then headed straight for the plate-glass window of the typing pool. Our saviour was the slope outside this window. The mangle ran up, somehow coming to a stop just inches away from the glass, through which a lot of horrified young women were staring.

As George and I ran up, it rolled down again towards the pavement and we grabbed it. Turning it round with a shouted, 'sorry', we ran as fast as we could with our clumsy, heavy burden until we got it home. A miracle happened that day, because no-one was hurt; God was on our side.

# 8

# *God Save the Queen*

February 1952 saw us studying for the dreaded scholarship. None of us wanted to pass as it would mean going to a grammar school. We did however want to do reasonably well and gain just enough points to go to Portswood Secondary Modern with distinction.

This was interrupted when our headmaster, Mr Huggins, unexpectedly came in to our classroom. We all stood but he waved us to be seated and there were tears in his eyes.

'As you are the senior class in the school you will be the first to be told. King George VI died peacefully in his sleep last night.'

I was transfixed at my desk, unable to grasp what my headmaster was telling me. The king was dead, surely not? This was the sort of thing that only happened in history lessons. It was of course only too true and his eldest daughter, Princess Elizabeth, was at that moment hurrying, with her husband Prince Philip, back home from South Africa to become Queen. This became an exciting time for us at school and we were all presented with beautiful mugs in preparation for the coronation of Queen Elizabeth II, which was to take place in 1953.

First though we had to sit the scholarship and this was done on the first two days of the summer holidays. It wasn't as frightening as I had led myself to believe and I did reasonably well. All of us did just enough to ensure we would be going to the senior section of our school to complete our education. With that done we could now really enjoy the summer holidays of 1952. They were the best yet with swimming, boating and cart racing taking priority, and we threw ourselves into every game with vigour.

John Bates got us to help him build a camp at the bottom of his garden. This was made with corrugated sheets of tin and, when we finished, it resembled an Eskimo's igloo. The entrance was so low we had to crawl along on all fours. The inner sanctum was a small but cosy little room into which we fitted with ease. This became our secret hideout. Although cleverly constructed, to call it this was really laughable.

John's house was right next to the bombed buildings and his back garden could easily be seen by anyone walking up the road. Which meant our camp could be too, so what on earth was secret about it? The only thing we didn't have was a neon sign with an arrow pointing down saying 'we are here'. When we were not running up and down making a general nuisance of ourselves, it was common knowledge that we could be found at either of our two camps. A second one was built at the bottom of Victor Warrender's garden; this was also in plain view.

Whenever we had a game in full swing, one or other of our mothers would appear with a bag and announce they wanted something from the shops. This happened to me so many times and I would have to break off and run up there. That is until the infamous day Mrs Priestly appeared and shouted to her eldest son Brian. The Priestly boys were always, to my mind, very disrespectful to their parents and referred to them as the old man and woman. None of the rest of us did this, always saying mother and father, or mum and dad.

So when Brian was asked to go to the shop, we were resigned to being one short, but he turned to his mother and said, 'Go yourself, I'm playing.' We stood in shock, waiting for Mrs Priestly's reaction. None of us, not even Pat Marriot, would dare say anything like this to our mothers. 'Oh you never do anything I ask you,' she said, then turned to her youngest son Peter who was also playing with us. She got the same answer here too, then to my utter disbelief came out of her house a few moments later carrying the shopping bag and went herself.

After seeing this I knew I had been doing it wrong all the time. All you needed to do to avoid these annoying interruptions is tell your mother to go herself. It wasn't long before I got the chance. I had landed the leading role in a cowboy game by shouting 'bags I Roy Rogers'. He was our hero and we had seen him in many films at the Savoy and the Palladium. So to be playing him gave you a status over everyone else. Just as I was busy organising a posse to go after the bandits, played by our very own baddies John Bates, Timmy Donaldson and, of course, Pat Marriot, my mother came out with a bag and called me to go to the shops.

Ready for this, I called back 'Go yourself, I'm playing.' There was a short and very ominous silence before my mother literally erupted. Not a large woman, she still exuded power and shouted loud enough for the whole area to hear. 'What did you say?'

With that she took two bounding steps and caught me by the scruff of my shirt collar. My feet didn't touch the ground as I was dragged indoors to the biggest hiding I had yet experienced. Never answer your parents back had been the watchword of my upbringing and I had broken this rule. I certainly didn't go out to play again that day and was reminded on several occasions of the perils of disobeying my mother. My mum and Mrs Priestly were two very different people and from that day on I showed her dutiful respect.

Preparations were going ahead, both in the news and in Belgrave Road, for the coronation of Queen Elizabeth II. For the second time in less than ten years the road would be decked with flags, and a huge party was being organised. Even though the big ceremony was not to take place until the spring of next year, 1953, it really was an exciting thing to experience.

Mr Aldridge, who acted as caretaker of Belgrave Church Hall, had organised two events. The first of these was a monthly social evening for every family in the road. The hall was already used for whist drives every other week and these were well attended. The social evenings were something different and made more enjoyable because Vickie Masterman was always there and my feelings for her were growing stronger all the time. Here I could get close to her and take part in the same games she did.

The Belgrave Road Boys Club was held every Thursday evening and these were a revelation. We didn't stay in the hall, but went out and visited the most exciting places. At the electricity power station we were given an extensive tour of the works. Here we saw enormous boilers, used to produce steam to power the plant. The man showing us around explained in detail the vital part they played in the operation, but also the consequences of running out of water. This was delivered very bluntly indeed with no thought about our feelings. Our guide simply shrugged his shoulders and said, 'If that happens they would blow up.' I was stunned and vowed there and then that at no time in my life would I have anything to do with boilers.

Visits were made to the fire station where we were allowed to sit behind the wheel of a real fire engine and speak on the two way radio linked up to the control room. We went to the airport at Swaythling and watched the planes coming and going, as well as, once again sitting at the controls, this time in the cockpit of one of the giant car carriers. These had fronts that opened fully, letting down a ramp for vehicles to drive on and off. They were called 'silver city' and we loved watching these giants. In those days the airport didn't have a concrete runway; planes took off and landed on grass, unlike today.

I felt slightly claustrophobic when we went to the docks. We had a ball until we were shown one of the old-fashioned rubber-diving suits. Air was pumped in and large weighted boots were worn on your feet for ballast. I was one of the boys picked to try on the helmet but as I went to put my head inside, a feeling of dread and fear came over me and nothing would pursued me to have another go.

One of the things we were most looking forward to was the landing of the flying boat. 'Here it is boys,' our guide shouted. We looked to where he was pointing and

Our first Bournemouth beach outing, with my family, August 1947.

My family all together in the back garden of the house in Belgrave Road.

Harold Brown's; where the owner would always see that you had enough.

This shows two blocks of six houses. My home, No. 94, is the one with the windows open, in the second block on the far left.

This is my memory of the shops as I grew up. Chandler's can be clearly seen in this picture, with Martin's butcher shop next door.

VE-Day celebrations with an undamaged shop in the background.

Portswood Road in the 1970s – changed greatly from where we would 'run for messages'.

The Waggoners Arms; one of the three pubs, in the area, my father would frequent.

Martin's butcher shop and Lowman's bakers, with the newsagents that replaced Chandler's in between.

Portswood Road; with the first ever B&Q store.

Upstream; showing the far bank of the River Itchen. The area in the background with the single dead tree is where we swam.

Two of the original Dyer's boats, now in the care of the St Denys Sailing and Rowing Club.

VE-Day celebrations; my mother and I are in the centre.

VE-Day celebrations; my mother is in the centre with the white-cross ribbon in her hair.

Belgrave Road as it was in my youth.

The author, James Marsh.

were disappointed because it was a seaplane. It made a perfect landing on the water, and while this was a thrilling sight, we had seen it many times before. Seaplanes made regular trips from Mayflower Park. The docks guide had used the correct name of flying boat, because they took off and landed on water. We had visualised a real boat, flying over the docks and coming in to land, but sadly this was not to be.

We enjoyed many other interesting trips and these culminated with a look around the nerve centre of Southampton, the Civic Centre. Will any of us who were there that day ever forget going up the clock tower? We trudged up those steps, then looked out the small windows to see so much of the town of our birth. The clock was about to strike and, standing right under the huge bell, our ears were ringing as it crashed out four times to let the citizens of Southampton know it was four o'clock in the afternoon.

The summer holidays were beginning to reach their conclusion and we would soon be starting on a new adventure in Senior School. Now young adults, this was starting to show in other directions as well. Until now I had considered girls to be good friends, alright at some things but hopeless at the rough and tumble games we sometimes played. They were no use at firing cap guns because they flinched at the bang when the trigger was pulled. At pirates they couldn't keep up with us, or when we repelled borders, and words failed me when trying to describe their swordplay.

But that year, two new games were introduced. In the game 'Mothers and Fathers' we always ended up being spanked; even on top of our clothing this was the kind of contact we had not had before. With 'Doctors and Nurses' we were even more adventurous and always had complaints below the waist, necessitating careful examination. It was all very tame because nothing was seen but underwear, but it was the girls who were seeing it.

There was the opportunity, if you were very lucky, to find a girl who would agree to show you her body. Much was my excitement when Bobby Westmore told me he had found just the girl to do this, and she was waiting for us in some bushes by the side of the recreation ground. I needed no persuasion and he and I rushed to the spot. She was indeed quite willing to take off her clothes for our enjoyment. We couldn't believe our luck, until the bomb hit. 'Of course you'll both have to take yours off as well,' she said, looking at us both.

Still steeped in a Victorian upbringing there was no way I could do this. So the chance was lost and my curiosity about girls went on until Edwin Whelan and I discovered the Grand Theatre. This was opposite the Civic Centre and we went many times, seeing some of the top stars of the stage. We found out there was to be a nude review in a few weeks and, after enquiring, were told there would be naked ladies on the stage. We waited with feverish excitement for the Saturday of the show to come round, and when it did we were right in the front of the queue.

Up in the balcony we waited for the curtain to go up then leaned so far out of our seats, it's a wonder we didn't fall. But where were the naked ladies we had waited such a long time to see? They were there, on the stage in front of us, but as a man sitting close by explained, they were not allowed to move about with no clothes on, but had to sit still behind some very cleverly positioned pillars. So all we saw of these ladies was a small piece of their bare arms and legs. A swizzle if there ever was one, and we left still not knowing what the naked female body looked like.

All too soon the day came when we had to go back to school, but not by the usual route. We now had to enter the senior boy's playground on the other side and we were very nervous about this. As juniors in this school the top boys would be so much older and bigger. We quickly learned to dodge them because they weren't above giving us nippers a rough time if they got the chance.

That first morning we met in the school hall and were introduced to the head-mistress, Mrs Shaft. She was a very fair and kindly woman, but strict when she needed to be. As we waited in a room that seemed enormous to us, she explained how the classes would be made up. The top class would be the art one, this was for boys and girls who had passed the scholarship and won a place. There would then be class one for girls, class two for boys and class three was mixed.

The divide between male and female was even more strictly adhered to in this school. Even in playground activity the boys were round the back whilst the girls played at the front, next to the infants and juniors. We both had our own entrances and weren't allowed to encroach on each other. No girls ever appeared in the boys' playground and vice versa. The entire Belgrave intake went into class two, with one exception and that was me. Suddenly all the boys I had grown-up with were in a different class and as most of the girls had gone to other schools, notably Vickie Masterman, who had gone to our archrivals, Swaythling School in Mayfield road, I was most put out. I felt alone and stranded in a place that should have felt familiar and in a class of boys and girls I didn't know, except for one.

Most of my new classmates had come from St Denys' Infants and Juniors and with them came Audrey. This was Aunt Ada's daughter, a cousin on my mother's side and one I knew very well as we were both the same age. Several times over the past years I had been to her house in Tennyson Road, Portswood for family gatherings and each time the fair came to Southampton we would meet up and go round together, before going back to Aunty's house for tea. I didn't know anybody else, but in a remarkably short space of time this changed.

Also in the hall that morning was the school's headmaster, Mr Lyme. A small man but not one to get on the wrong side of, his office was on the top floor and to be sent here meant you were in for a punishment. Mrs Shaft's office was on the ground floor in the long corridor leading to the hall. In class that morning I met not only new boys who would become close friends, but also a rival for Vickie's place in my heart. Her name was Janet Moss and all the boys noticed her at once. But in the four years we were in that class not one of us ever got close enough to Janet to become really friendly, although we tried. This could be down, in part, to that

Victorian divide between the sexes that was so much more in evidence than in the juniors. At least there we had all played together.

We most definitely did not have PT, short for Physical Training, or games together. For either of these lessons we would have to change, and the removal of any of our clothing was not permitted within sight of the opposite sexes. The boys had to change into vests and shorts, which at least looked alright when out on the sports field. But the girls had to wear blouses tucked into the most unglamorous navy-blue knickers. If we had wanted to see girls' underwear, when we were a bit younger, these would have put us off for life. For these two lessons the boys of the art class joined us, while our girls joined theirs; in this way we got to know each other and more friendships developed.

In class three that first morning, I met two of the boys, with whom I would become best friends, they were Malcolm Tizzard and Michael Dibben. Michael lived in St Denys in South Road; which was in easy reach of the River Itchen. I played here a lot with him from 1952 onwards because it gave me the best of both worlds. We already had our own part of the river at the back of our houses, but this was further down under the railway bridge that carried the Portsmouth line. None of us in Belgrave knew this part of the river because we had not had the chance of exploring here before.

It was the St Denys' boys' territory and we were not welcome. At no time when we were hiring Dyer's boats were we allowed to come down either. Mr Dyer was always most firm about this.

'You can go up river, but don't ever let me catch you going down. The currents are too strong so you don't go there in my boats,' he would say, glaring at us.

In this he was most determined and we had learned to recognise when a grown-up was giving us a direct order that was not to be disobeyed. The St Denys' boys, however, knew it intimately and regularly swam under the railway bridge. They accepted me without any trouble because I was a school friend of Michaels and I swam and played with them all.

The river here was surrounded by prefabs and there were a lot of these in Southampton at the time. A throw back from the war, these were prefabricated houses, put up in a hurry to house the many families whose homes had been destroyed by the German bombs. They lasted longer than anyone expected and were still being lived in well into the sixties.

Our first playtime arrived and we all came out with one thought in mind, to run round the back of the L-shaped playground where there was a gate with a small flight of stone steps leading down to the infants' area. Many times we had come back from summer holidays to see boys who were now seniors crowding into this gateway, poking fun at the little boys still in the juniors. Now it was our turn and we enjoyed pointing and laughing, without a thought that just a few weeks ago we had been there ourselves.

When we went into the hall for PT it was necessary to get changed and there was another condition waiting to be met. We had to change from our school clothes into vest and shorts, and there was a time limit for this to be completed. Our sports master showed no emotion at all and told us that any boy taking longer than this allotted time to change and get into line ready for the start of the lesson would lose house marks.

Portswood Senior School was divided into four houses: Nelson, Drake, Shakespeare and Livingstone. I was in Livingstone house and every Wednesday morning at the house meeting Mr Weatheral, the school music teacher and Livingstone house master, would tell us how we were doing and if we were in line for the top house prize. We were expected to gain points for good work and not lose them for any reason.

When the boys of my class and the art boys were waiting outside to go in for the next PT lesson, every item of clothing that could be decently removed was discarded. Things like shoes and socks, jackets, shirts, ties etc. It must have resembled a strip tease act, but we did it so as not to be late in line for the lesson. Our PT and sports master was Mr Cookson and he was a revelation, as he showed us a lot of sports we wouldn't otherwise have been involved in.

One of these was Shinty, a Scottish game played in the boy's playground using sticks and a ball. Mr Cookson roared at us not to use them to stop opponents gaining ground on our goal. A waste of time, we were all as bad as one another and as soon as one of the other side broke free one or other of us would trip them up. The same thing was done to us as well so everything evened out. We went back into lessons with scraped knees and elbows and would have to go and see 'Dr Drop 'Em' who looked after the seniors as well.

We also played rounders, a game we were used to because we played a lot on the bombed buildings at home. But Mr Cookson changed the rules a bit. The bat we could usually hold in one hand had trebled in size and was as big, if not bigger, than most of us. As we looked at him in total surprise he told us it was about time we learned to play the real game

'This boys, is a baseball bat and from today we are going to play the American game.'

This was all very well but some of us, and this certainly included me, could hardly raise this bat, let alone use it. But after some instruction we managed, and had the greatest fun playing. We all threw the small rounders bat behind us as we ran but now we had to get used to not doing it because this one was big enough to break a leg if it hit anyone.

Mr Michealson was a very strict disciplinarian and none of us dared misbehave in his class. But he was a marvellous teacher for all that. He was our science master and we had some very interesting experiments. The most memorable of these being the day he brought a bucket of water into class. A two shilling piece was dropped in and all we had to do to get our hands on this fortune was reach into the bucket and grab it.

What Mr Michealson failed to tell us however was that he had wired it up to the electricity supply so a small charge was now running through the bucket. As I watched boy after boy try and fail to get their hands on the money, I decided they were being too slow. If you plunged your hand straight in and made a quick grab you wouldn't feel any electric. As soon as my hand touched the surface of the water though, it went up my arm making me jump back in shock. Electricity and water don't mix and even with just a small charge Mr Michelson's money was quite safe.

All of us had to go regularly to the hated swimming baths for lessons and it was Mr Michealson who took us. Soon after the electricity trick he was on duty and before we started he sternly told us to be careful because he didn't want to be splashed. But as we were drawing to the end of our lesson one boy got into difficulties and started to go down. Mr Michealson shouted to two of the boys who were still in the water to help him, but they failed to hear and did nothing. Then before our startled eyes our teacher dived in fully clothed and went to the aid of the stricken boy. How well we enjoyed the rest of that day, the drowning boy was none the worse and we had to stay at the swimming baths while our teacher's clothes dried out.

Mrs Hawton was our form teacher in that first year and she was a great hit with all of us; her specialty was drama. She would hand out a play, delegate parts and then we would start to read it. Inevitably mistakes were made and she would interrupt and explain to us what the problem was. If we continued to get it wrong however she would take the book from us and read the part herself to show how it should be performed. Even at our age we recognised the talent this lady had for acting. Over the next four years we regularly, and quite deliberately, got our parts wrong so that our teacher would take over and do it herself. Then we would sit back and enjoy her performance.

There was also our woodwork teacher Mr Bevan, a man I never took to. Even though he gave us the skills we needed, his method left a great deal to be desired. He would lecture us about the proper use of tools, such as planes and chisels, and the proper way to make joints. If anyone got it wrong though, instead of speaking to the individual and explaining his mistake, he would take the boy responsible for it by the ear. Squeezing painfully, the rest of the class would be called round the unfortunate boy's bench

'Right, show us how you made this mess then.' With flaming cheeks the whole miserable mistake would have to be played out. A very embarrassing way to do things and none of us liked him for it.

Opposite the woodwork room was the domestic science or cookery class as we called it. Boys were only taught things they could do with their hands so they could go out to work and become breadwinners. Girls learned cooking and needlework, things that were used in the care of the home so they could become housewives. Not only were boys not allowed in the girl's playground, but the cookery and needlework rooms were also out of bounds. It was also taboo for girls to come anywhere near the woodwork, plastic-work or metalwork rooms. Indeed we even had our own entrances in and out of school. Boys and girls could not even share the same desks. These were designed to seat two side-by-side, but never at any time would this be by a boy and a girl.

Rules were strictly administered and had to be obeyed, under threat of severe punishment, and no-one was better suited to mete this out than our new headmaster, Mr Lyme. For any breach the culprits were called into his study to have at least three strokes of the cane across each hand, and boy did it hurt. He brought the cane down from over his head and the stinging effect will never be forgotten by any of us.

We didn't like it at the time but it taught us the difference between right and wrong. I was once caned for playing on the school steps and got the usual three on each hand. My fellow sufferer that day was a boy who had to put up with a lot of verbal abuse because we thought he was stupid. Even in the seniors he still couldn't read or write. The school did all they could but it was a common sight to see him trying to make sense of a baby book. When I last saw him, in 1956, he still couldn't write his own name. None of us or our teachers had heard of dyslexia; nothing was known back then about things like this, and certainly no help was available. He did fortunately go on to lead a productive adult life.

On Christmas day 1952, Edwin Whelan came over to our house and the two of us were in the front room. This was used only on very special occasions, at all other times none of us were permitted to go inside. But this was Christmas and so we were able to spend those two days here. Tastefully decorated, with plenty to eat and drink and a big fire burning, this was indeed heaven. We were having a great time when I spotted a full bottle of whiskey on the top of the sideboard.

We had been going to the cinema regularly and loved to watch cowboy films. As I gazed at that bottle I remembered how our heroes pushed their way through the bat-wing doors of the saloon, then strode up the bar and loudly demanded whiskey. They always got a full glass which they would raise to their mouth and gulp down in one. Although still only twelve years old, and wearing the traditional short trousers of boyhood, we had started trying to be men. We smoked and managed to buy five woodbines between us whenever we were out of sight of home. Anything that made us feel grown-up we did, so despite Edwin's warning I poured a very generous tot of whiskey into a glass.

Now, standing as my cowboys did, I lifted the glass to my mouth. Will I ever forget the shock of that raw spirit? I had no idea that something could taste so awful and burn my mouth at the same time. I forgot all about being manly and wanted to rid myself of this vile tasting liquid. Instinctively I turned to the fireplace and spat it straight into the fire. The result could have devastating. A huge fireball erupted from the grate and shot up the chimney, but somehow failed to set it alight. I was the luckiest boy around that day, because I could have been responsible for setting fire to my own home.

Spring of 1953 will never be forgotten by anyone who was in this country at the time. This was because of the Coronation of Queen Elizabeth II. For weeks leading up to this wondrous occasion we had been busy preparing, both at home and school. Belgrave Road was again decked out with flags and a street party was arranged. There was a school holiday and we were all presented with Coronation mugs. I wonder if any of us still has theirs – I don't and can't even remember what happened to it. They were blue with a picture of her majesty on the front, and every school boy and girl in England got one to take home.

Just before the big day dawned another wondrous event took place. Edmund Hillary and Sherpa Tenzing reached the summit of the previously unconquerable Everest, and man stood for the first time on top of this huge mountain. I was just old enough to appreciate the importance of these two momentous occasions.

The day of the Coronation was wonderful. We listened to it on the wireless and then sat down at the trestle tables to enjoy a street party put on by our mothers. The pictures of the Queen actually being crowned were seen a couple of days later at the cinema on Pathe News. It made us proud to be British as we watched the beautiful gold Coronation coach, being drawn by six horses to Westminster Abbey. Just a few days after, we were again at the cinema, this time with the school. All of us had been taken to the Broadway in a fleet of buses to see the film of the conquering of Everest.

Momentous changes were happening all around us. The world was starting to recover from the awful war years and the aftermath that had left so many towns and cities in ruins. Southampton's High Street, which had been flattened during the Blitz, was temporarily rebuilt, all with single-storey shops. One day mum brought the bread home as usual and I started to unwrap it. I was surprised to see that it had greaseproof paper instead of the usual tissue. As I struggled to get the paper off mum shouted at me not to, telling me this bread is already sliced. What on earth can she mean by that? She was right. A quick investigation showed that the bread only had to be taken out slice by slice as needed.

Also, much to our relief we could now get tinned cat food. Chandler's, where we were still registered for our rations, had started to stock this new product. Now we had two cats to feed, Blitz and Timmy, who both had plum jam all through the week. Timmy really amused us as he ate his because he used his paw to spear the pieces of bread before lifting them to his mouth. But on Saturdays they still had their treat of cooked fish. Both of them went frantic during the cooking of this and mum couldn't put it down fast enough for them. Now it was simply open the tin to feed the cats, and they loved it.

At school we were required to learn new skills. In the case of PT this meant climbing ropes and wall bars. The first of these was no problem – being a skinny boy shimming up a rope was easy for me. I thought wall bars would be straight forward too. It was simplicity itself to clamber up, wrap your legs around the bars and hang upside down from the top. There was no danger of falling because your legs were hard up against the wall behind. So we were very smug about it.

Mr Cookson told us that wall bars were to be treated with respect and to do it correctly he intended to give us a demonstration. We, of course, didn't need it because we had scrambled to the top with absolute ease. He looked at us and read the conceit in our faces.

'Alright then,' he said 'now we'll do it properly.'

With that he walked over and undid a bolt that went from the floor to the top of the bars, and hadn't been seen by any of us. With us watching closely he proceeded to pull them away so they ended up across the hall, at right angles to the wall. Now we had to climb again, and gone was the smug self-esteem we had been feeling before. With no support from behind we had only our legs wrapped around the top bar to stop us from falling. It took us some time to get used to this, but as I was starting to excel at PT I managed it sooner than most.

The few of us who did it best, and this included my best friends Michael Dibben and Malcolm Tizzard, were watched closely and as a result always picked to appear in PT displays that were put on for our parents. These were on the Open Days at the end of the summer term and at Christmas. For this we needed to be good at everything: rope climbing, wall bars and vaulting over the old wooden horse.

The displays were very exciting and wonderful for us to be involved with. Mr Cookson decided to make it even better with the introduction of a pyramid. This meant four boys kneeling on the floor, three more would kneel on their backs, followed by two at the next level. One boy would then run from the corner of the room, mount the pyramid and stand triumphantly at the top. I got this glamorous job and would be the centre of attention as I stood proudly aloft.

Both Malcolm and Michael had a part to play because they, along with one or two others, were very good at doing handstands. Four boys were to perform these up against the pyramid. This was practiced so many times before the performance that on the day it went off perfectly, and was received with warm applause from the assembled parents. The joy and pride I felt as I stood on my lofty perch while a photograph was taken is beyond description.

On the last day of the summer term, as we were leaving to go home, Mr Cookson gave each of us a copy of the pyramid photograph. I was so eager to see it I didn't wait until I got home before tearing open the envelope. My mother, who knew nothing about the photograph, would be as pleased as I was seeing her clever son as the star of the school PT display. She would buy a frame then hang it on the wall in the kitchen for everyone to see – that is after she had been around to all the neighbours to show them.

I looked in horror at the photograph and stood in shock. My blood ran cold because the fact that I was a skinny boy was shown up in all its gory detail. For displays we were not required to wear vests, only gym shoes and socks with black shorts. As I stood bare-chested at the top of the pyramid, with both of my arms outstretched, my ribs stood out like beacons, and made every other part of me look skinny. Needless to say mum never got to see that photograph. I tore it up in disgust and worried for some time over the state of my body.

Talking this over with Edwin Whelan we both decided to send off for one of the most popular body building kits available at the time. This was by an American, who presumably had once been a seven stone weakling. Then he discovered dynamic tension and built his body up so much that he won the Mr Universe title. The advertisement for this, that appeared regularly in newspapers, magazines and comics of the day, showed a thin man on the beach with his girlfriend. When a big muscle man comes along and accidentally kicks sand in his face, he turns to his girlfriend and says, 'Don't worry I'll get even with that bully some day.'

Whereupon the girl says, 'Oh, don't bother junior', and goes off to have fun with Mr Muscles, who parades around the beach with a girl hoisted on each of his shoulders. The disgruntled boyfriend goes home, sees the advert and sends for it. Then, just two weeks later, he too is sporting big biceps and goes down to the beach, punches the bully on the jaw and wins back the love and admiration of his girlfriend.

I'm afraid this didn't work out for Edwin and I. We spent hours following the method of making one set of muscles work against another. Pushing an arm or a leg downwards, the corresponding limb would be lifted in the opposite direction, creating tension that was supposed to make our muscles grow bigger. We never did go to the beach to receive admiring glances from the girls. At the end of that summer holiday Edwin and I had been at it every day for six weeks and could see absolutely no difference. The course ended up in the dustbin.

Midway through 1953 we moved up a year and were now in class 7, where our form master was the much liked Mr Green. He was a wonderful teacher and such a kindly man. We learnt so much because we paid strict and avid attention to everything he taught us. Now in our second year, and twelve years old, most of the boys in the class had achieved their greatest goal in life so far. They had moved from short trousers and were now wearing the long trousers that signified manhood.

This was such an important milestone in every boy's life and I, along with my two brothers George and Ron, was due for a new suit. As I was nearly thirteen, I convinced myself my parents would take this into account and buy me one with long trousers. The disappointment when this didn't happen was paramount. The new grey flannel suit I was presented with had the usual short ones. I was so unhappy, but still of course had to thank my parents properly for the new clothes.

Michael Dibben had gone one better than the rest of us and not only had long trousers, but had somehow got his mother to buy him a pair of the latest craze in mens and boys' wear, denim jeans. He was wearing these when he called for me to go to school some days later. As he rode his bike into Belgrave Road he was delighted to see that it was flooded. Eagerly he rode at this, meaning to spray water out on both sides as he went through. I would have told him it was too deep but it was too late, he found out for himself.

His bike stopped dead in the middle of the flood water and just fell over sideways, dumping Michael and his new jeans into the water. He came out soaking wet and had to go home and change into short trousers before coming to school that day. Just a few weeks after, I came home from school to be told, that a parcel had come so I went upstairs to see what this could be.

Entering the bedroom I stopped dead and stared because lying on my bed was a pair of long trousers. I spun around and found my mother standing in the doorway smiling at me

'Yes,' she said, 'they're for you.' Never have I changed from one pair of trousers to another so quickly, and then it was out into the road as I strutted up and down. 'Look at me' my posture shouted, 'I'm in long trousers, I've grown-up.'

The amusing thing was that, I immediately looked down on some of my friends, boys I had only just walked home with that very day, because they were still in shorts and were now mere babies. Silly perhaps, but it was understandable, because long trousers were such a huge step forward in every boy's life. The photograph of Mr Green's class of 1953, which has me in the front row next to Michael Dibben, shows every boy in the class had by then passed through this stage and was wearing long trousers.

Sitting next to me in this photo is a boy who was a rival for anything Pat Marriot ever got up to. His name was Dennis Armond and he was part of a very large family who ran a second-hand shop in Portswood Road, by the Catholic church. Dennis was a real tear away and got up to some really wild and reckless escapades in the short time he was with us at school.

Among these was the day he climbed, with another boy, onto the roof of the school and set about stealing the lead. A constant thorn in the side of our headmaster, Mr Lyme, he never missed an opportunity to embarrass him. This ranged from aiming water bombs from one high vantage point or another, to sabotaging his car. Inevitably this behaviour, coupled with constant truancy, led to him being involved with the police. He was with us for two years then sent to an approved school. We heard nothing of him after that but in later years I met him again. I found out that while at this school he was taken in hand by a master who taught him to swim to a high degree of efficiency. He now owns his own swimming pool and, with his wife, runs swimming lessons for youngsters in Southampton.

# 9

# *Goodbye Schooldays*

Ron had started school and it was my job to see that he got home safely. Here, I was not the cruel brother I was, when at home. We had one major road to cross and I took my duties very seriously. I might have been extremely mean to Ron at times, but as far as his safety was concerned I cut no corners. Whether I liked it or not he was my brother and blood really is thicker than water. I did the same for Jean when it was her turn to start, even though this only lasted a few months as I was coming up to school-leaving age by then.

I had quite a shock one time when I came downstairs and recognised the man standing in our hall. It was our Hawks Speedway idol, Dan Higgs, and he was waiting for my sister, Pat. Now almost grown-up, we didn't make the huge fuss we would have done in previous years whenever we had something to tell the others. But on this day I completely forgot about that and ran eagerly up the road to tell them that Dan Higgs was not only in our house, but going out with my sister. Predictably no-one believed me but I was ready for that and simply waited. Sure enough, not ten minutes later, he emerged from No.94 with my sister on his arm. I looked at the others with a self-satisfied smirk on my face that said it all.

As we were now nearly thirteen our attention turned to part-time jobs. For most of the others this meant becoming paper boys. We weren't supposed to work until we had passed our fourteenth birthday, but in those days we could get away with it. There were two paper shops in the area, Wintrage's and Bailie's, and most of the Belgrave boys worked out of the former. But Edwin Whelan got his round from Bailie's. I did this for him when he had a cold and didn't like it at all. For the sum of 5s a week, the walking and carrying that had to be done in all weathers was quite frankly not worth it.

I was very pleased when my brother George won a Scholarship that took him to Deanery School down by the docks. The only one of us to achieve this, it would ultimately lead to him gaining an apprenticeship at Thorneycroft's shipyard in Woolston – the start of a great career in engineering that George has enjoyed over many years since.

This paved the way for me to take over as butcher's boy to Ted Martin at the shop where mum bought our meat, a job that paid a whole pound a week. The day I started will always be imprinted on my mind. I was greeted by Mr Martin, 'So you're George's brother are you? Well you'll have to ******* well shape up or you'll be ******* well out.'

I was not just shocked but paralysed. I had never heard language like this before. At school we were always taught to speak the King's English and nothing else, with slogans like 'manners maketh the man'. We had been taught the value of better dressing and the way to behave at all times when in the company of other people. But here and now I was hearing words I didn't know existed. George had not said a word about it to me, preferring to let me find out for myself, as he had done.

My duties were to take the deliveries out every day on a bicycle with a cage in front of the handlebars. Then at dinnertimes it was up to the bank on Portswood Junction to get change. On Mondays all the takings from the previous week's trading had to be paid in – a small boy peddling along Portswood Road with something like £150 in a bag pushed inside my shirt. If anyone had known about these regular Monday trips I am sure I would have encountered violence at one time or another, even though things like that were rare in those days.

In the evenings it was clear up the shop, wash the trays that had been used to display meat, scrub the block on which it had been chopped and sweep sawdust from the floor. On Saturdays, after delivery, all the fat that Mr Martin cut off animal carcasses during the week had to be minced up, a back breaking and extremely boring job. The next morning, down in the cellar, this was put into a clean dustbin then set on an old gas stove to be melted down and sold during the week as dripping. Because it was seven days a week, this job was very well paid and I got used to it all except for one part.

Mr Martin was an alcoholic, which I didn't understand because none of the people in my life were like this. My Father went to the pub every night but never came home drunk. Merry, yes; he would promise you the earth and mean it. But once he slept off the alcohol he never remembered a thing. We were used to this and found it amusing, but now I found out what real drinking was all about.

He always opened at around five o'clock in the morning and did a full day, never closing before six o'clock in the evening. As soon as the shop door was shut and locked he went straight down the Brook Inn for his nightly large helpings of gin. During the day, whenever I was in the shop, it was 'right nipper, medicine.' On no account was Mrs Martin to know, so the first thing he asked was 'Where is she?'

And if she was not in the shop but in their private quarters at the back, we would disappear into the walk-in freezer where a bottle went into the pocket under my white plastic apron.

Then it was down to the Brook, and into the Bottle and Jug, for Mr Martin's medicine. The bar staff of course knew exactly what this was and went to the optics to put a double gin into it. Not legal even then for a boy my age to be served with alcohol, but Martin's boys had been coming here for years. They knew who it was for and that we would be back many more times during each day to fetch it.

I handed over about 8/-, then it was back to the shop and into the freezer where the bottle was passed from my pocket to his. But not for long; with a final look to make sure his wife was not in view, it was off with the top and the gin was downed in one. Time and time again this procedure was repeated but he was never out-wardly drunk. Quite how he managed to wield that large cleaver will always be a mystery to me. The prepared meat in the window was usually gone by lunchtime, so when a customer came into the shop in the afternoon, anything they wanted had to be cut for them.

The air turned blue whenever he cut himself and he glared at the blood running over his hands. This he cured by wrapping gauze round the offending finger before carrying on. If two chops were requested one would be the size of three while the other was so thin it resembled a rasher of bacon. He had an answer for most things that came up. In an incident involving my sister, Pat, who had gone in to complain that the joint of beef she had been served the week before had not cooked properly and tasted awful, he simply looked at her and said, 'God sent the meat my dear, the Devil sent the bad cooks.' There was no answer to that and she just turned and left the shop.

He was outrageous with most of the female customers, saying things I didn't understand at first.

'I did it on the kitchen table,' one of them would say, talking about the house-work.

'That must have been uncomfortable, it's better on the floor,' he'd say roaring with laughter.

'Oh you're awful, what if my husband heard you?' This just made him laugh even more.

'Tell them to come and ask me about it and I'll show them how it's done.'

In the two years or so I worked for Ted Martin I learned more about life than at any other time. For instance it was he who told me where babies actually come from, and he described the sex act in great detail. He told it in a way that excited me and made me long for the days when I could expect this sort of thing to happen in my life. He taught me to swear like a trooper when things went wrong, but never to do this in the presence of a woman. I learned how to be cheeky but not offensive, artful but not dishonest, and the meaning of punctuality and hard work.

I fell out with him only once. Every dinner time I would run up to the shop after my meal. Then, taking the money in bank notes, would pedal up to the bank for change. When I got back he put each bag onto the shop scales because he knew exactly how much they should weigh. But on this day one of the bags was light.

'This one's short,' he said and glared at me. I put my hand into my trouser pocket and found a two shilling piece that had fallen out. I thought nothing of this and just handed the coin to him with an apology then went back to school.

When I came home that evening I rushed my tea as usual to get to the shop as quickly as possible. Mum told me I wouldn't have to do that tonight, nor ever again because Mr Martin didn't want me working for him anymore. I was stunned and looked dumbfounded at my mother.

'What have you done to bring this about?' she asked, and I couldn't tell her because I didn't know myself.

The next day when I was at school she went and asked him herself. I got home that evening to a grim reception. Ted Martin told her I tried to steal two shillings from him and he wouldn't employ anyone who did that sort of thing. My mother had taught us all about the evils of stealing and I only tried it once.

With the rest of the gang we thought we were clever the time we distracted Mr Whitlock and stole a bag of sweets to eat on the way to school. Our wave of crime only lasted two days. We were caught; each of us got a well-deserved smack on the ear and was told if anything like this happened again our parents would be informed. In our house the rules were even more strictly observed. Never touch anything that doesn't belong to you. This included the mail; if it didn't have your name on the envelope then it wasn't for you and you didn't touch it.

By the time I worked for Martin's I had learned this lesson well and never attempted to take anything that wasn't mine. I was angry and deeply hurt by this insinuation. It was an accident and I told my mother in no uncertain way. She heard the sincerity in my voice and the next day went down to the butcher shop again. What she said to him I never found out but the next evening I was told not to linger over my tea because if I did I would be late for my job. From there, I looked forward to the day when I would leave school and start out on my own, working and earning my own living, making my own decisions and having an independent lifestyle.

At the end of the 1954 summer holidays, I realised this would be my last full year at Portswood School. The procedure then was if anyone reached the required age of fifteen before the start of the Christmas break they could leave then. As I was born on 6 December, I only had a year and a half to go. Now, very much seniors in the school, we ranked high in the playground.

Our science teacher, the much liked and deeply respected Mr Michealson, had left. We had no idea who his replacement would be and sat in absolute dismay when the formidable figure of our headmaster, Mr Lyme, entered the room. For almost three years this man had been the symbol of absolute authority, with no quarter being given if anyone broke the rules. Everyone left his study with either stinging hands or painful bottoms, depending upon the offence committed. We were dreading this, but how wrong we all were.

Up until now we had only known Mr Lyme the strict headmaster; now we were introduced to Mr Lyme the teacher, and the difference was phenomenal. His passion was for cars and for the whole year he taught us on that subject. The mysteries of the internal combustion engine were explained in detail and he took time with each boy. This was another lesson we shared with the art class. He made it so interesting that before long we were looking forward to his lesson each week, and many boys in that class benefited so much from his tutelage.

The motor car was beginning to come more and more into its own, with many families now owning one; so to be able to find out how the engines worked and how to repair one was worthwhile knowledge. I thought I already knew our headmaster, but in that school year of 1954/55 I was introduced to one of the most likeable and dedicated teachers of my schooldays. As we approached the end of the year he had a great treat in store; we were given a note for our parents to sign, giving permission to go on a school trip. We were told to get these back as soon as possible and, on the day in question, to bring sandwiches. Arriving at school we found a coach waiting for us after assembly.

Once aboard we were told our destination, the 1955 Motor Show at London's Earls Court. We had seen newsreels of this event at the cinema, where all the very latest cars from this country and around the world were on display, but to actually be there was amazing. I stepped out of the coach and looked in awe at the enormous and very impressive building. We went from stand to stand in that huge arena and sat in so many wonderful new cars, from the formal Rolls Royce to the very latest in smart, fast, sports cars. Even though we had to write an essay about this afterwards, it was very worthwhile.

In woodwork I was making progress. I had made small things like toast racks, magazine racks and breadboards, which were ready to take home in just a week or two. Now this year I went completely the other way. There was a catalogue in the woodwork room with pictures and instructions. Looking through this I stopped at a page showing an ironing board. Why I selected this I have no idea, but as soon as I saw it I knew I wanted to have a go at making one.

When I took the catalogue to Mr Bevan he scoffed at me. 'This will take time Marsh, and a lot more skill than you've got.' It was the sneering way he said it, coupled with the fact I had never liked this man, that made me dig in and stand up to him.

'Nevertheless, Sir,' I replied, looking straight back at him, 'I'd like the chance to try.'

'Right, try by all means but remember I warned you, this is way out of your league.'

He was so nearly right; that ironing board took me the whole of the school year to complete, as I battled with planes and joint making, often going wrong and having to do it all over again. What kept me going was the support of the rest of the class, who were willing me to succeed, and the smirk on Mr Bevan's face every time I made a mistake. When I found that a part didn't fit after weeks of preparing it, the disappointment was felt by everyone. Each time, I put up with the 'I told you so' looks from Mr Bevan and started again until I got it right.

As the end of that year approached I was nearly ready and my ironing board was looking the part. The legs now balanced so that it stood level. This had taken me weeks of despair to get right, one set of legs always ended up shorter than the other. The flat-top surface was smooth and ready to take any amount of ironing. There was a little square at the back end with asbestos lining for the hot iron to be placed when not in use. The bolts were firmly in place and there was just one final test before my prize would be ready to take home. It had to have the approval of the woodwork teacher.

It wasn't just me who stood with bated breath as Mr Bevan approached. He stood looking for a few moments as I stood timidly next to it, then, to my absolute horror, he hoisted his backside and placed one ample side of his body onto the flat top. There was a gasp all around the room, because everyone was watching and willing me to come through.

As his weight descended the board gave a creak and an ominous groan, and I turned away in despair. A whole year's work was going to be crushed by this ruth-less, unfeeling and spiteful man. In that moment I hated him with a passion I didn't know I had. I waited for the inevitable crash as the board collapsed, but incredibly this never came. When the teacher got off it stood as proudly as before.

There was silence around the room, followed almost immediately by a round of spontaneous cheering. When this noise finally subsided Mr Bevan really surprised me. He smiled then held out his hand. 'Well done Marsh, that's a very fine job.'

Another lesson had been learned. As I shook his hand I realised he had pushed me deliberately, and was responsible for the way I had battled to make that ironing board. The important thing had been to prove to myself and to him that I could do it. Time and again I was told things were beyond my capability, and each time I rose to the challenge.

It also brought me a little closer to my father because I now had the idea of taking up carpentry for a career. To speak to him on any subject up until then had been difficult to say the least. My mother followed the principles of the Victorian era and, because he was the family breadwinner, he became, for us at least, almost unapproachable. He lived for his work and this was all that really mattered to him.

He was out all hours as he worked in the building trade, and was earning the enormous sum of ten pounds a week, making us one of the well off families in the road. This was paid because so many men were needed in this vital industry.

Southampton, like every other large town or city in the country was being rebuilt after the devastation of the war. Gone were so many of the bomb sites we had played in, as new buildings were going up everywhere. In many places this meant the prefabricated houses we had played by in St Denys.

These were like caravans and were easy and quick to put together. They were only meant to last a year or two until real houses could be built, but the sheer scale of this task meant they lasted well into the sixties. When my grandparents were moved from their home in Mayfield Road in 1959, they were moved to one of these. For the first time I saw what they were like inside. For two people they were very comfortable, and they lived there until my gran died in 1963.

This was the second time I had approached him about my career prospects. Some weeks before I had obtained the address of a racing stable. Being very much on the small and skinny side, I saw myself becoming a jockey, so I wrote to this address and was actually offered an interview. Eagerly I showed this letter to dad, who was hugely unimpressed. To him, having a proper job bringing in a regular wage was all important.

'A jockey, nipper,' he exploded. 'What the hell is the use of that? Do you know what your chances are of getting anywhere in that business? Practically nil, don't waste your time.'

To say I was disappointed was putting it mildly, but he was my father so I didn't argue and didn't go for the interview. In the years since I have read many books by leading jockeys and realised he was probably right. I had no skill with horses and up to that time had not ridden one without assistance. So anyone with horse skills would have been way ahead of me. Had I tried I would probably have ended up with the job of a stable lad, mucking out and looking after two horses a day. The nearest I would have got to racing would be leading one or the other of these around the paddock.

Showing him the ironing board, I asked about the chances of my becoming a carpenter. This was received much more positively.

'A carpenter eh, nipper? Now there's a good trade to be in. As soon as you leave school I'll do my best to get you an apprenticeship with a good firm. That's a trade boy, and if you do well you'll be set up for life.' So all I needed to do now was finish out my school days.

In that final year we were challenged when our arch rivals, the boys of Swaythling School, gave notice that some of our lads had said things they weren't going to ignore. The result being that at lunch break, when most of our boys were on the playing fields of Portswood recreation ground – right next to our playground – a cry went up. 'The Swaythling boys are coming.' Indeed they were, a large crowd of them heading towards our playing fields.

The result was immediate; every boy from our school heeded the call and swarmed out to meet them. Massed in the road we started to shout taunts and insults at each other. Relentlessly the two sides moved closer and closer together until, with loud shouts, battle was joined. Several hundred boys now locked together as fists and feet were used to batter the other side into submission. It was difficult from the start to know whether the boy you were lashing out at was from our school or theirs, there was such a crush of boys involved. This was a fierce battle between two really equal sides. The Swaythling area had many families with hard reputations and when the Belgrave boys had gone into their territory as very young lads, we knew they would give us a hard time if they saw us there.

Now though, they were on our patch. If they got by us, our playing fields and, heaven forbid, our playground, would be at their mercy. We had our own hard-cases that came, not just from the Portswood area, but from all over Southampton. Although most of our boys had never even seen Swaythling School, they knew of the bitter rivalry between us. This was why we would have fought to the last one standing, if necessary, to keep these particular boys away from our school.

Kitchener Road was one of the better areas of Southampton, known to us as the posh road. A lot of the householders had telephones and, alarmed that such a large gathering of boys were now engaged in a very rowdy brawl, more than one of them had put in a call. With the fight in full swing the cry of 'Police' suddenly rent the air and both sides broke off, turned and ran full pelt to the safety of their own play-grounds. We looked a sorry sight, with torn clothes and lots of cuts and bruises. The satisfaction for us though was that the Swaythling boys had suffered just as much and looked no better than we did.

We got back in time for afternoon school and the only thing that happened was a visit in each classroom by the headmistress. Mrs Shaft told us the police had advised the school that they were aware of the riot and they would be out patrol-ling the roads around the two schools to prevent any repetition of this behaviour. Most of us had to face the anger of our mothers. Our school clothes were difficult for them to supply and my shirt and trousers were ripped. I looked a real sight, with a black eye and various other injuries and mum really tore into me. My defence that, 'It was the Swaythling boys who started it', went unheeded and I felt the full weight of her hand.

The next morning after assembly the girls were told to file out first as usual. But as we started to move the loud voice of Mr Lyme rang out, 'All the boys will remain.' We looked nervously at each other as we stood waiting, then Mrs Shaft glared at us. Never in all her years of teaching had so many boys let down the name of the school. Leaving the grounds to go and brawl in public, frightening the residents of Kitchener Road and involving her in a police enquiry. All our parents would be receiving a letter about their son's behaviour, and if any boy did anything like this again, then swift and very decisive punishment would follow.

All through this though we heard the pride in her voice, because although what we did was wrong the reason for it was not. It was our school and we were prepared to fight for it. No way were Swaythling boys ever going to get the chance to set foot on our recreation fields, let alone our playground. We were proud of Portswood School and every one of us showed it that day. For the following two weeks we wore our injuries with pride; they were gained in a battle for our school and we looked on them as badges of honour.

Things were changing all around me. The Belgrave gang I had grown-up with were now teenagers. As such we had given up our right to the bombed buildings and this was taken over by the younger children. Among these were Ron and Jean. In true Belgrave fashion they repelled 'Indians' and pirates from this hallowed playground. It was they who now paddled in the flood waters of the Spring tides. And it was they who flew down the slaughter house slope on their makeshift orange-box carts.

Here they were more adventurous than we had been, going a long way up Mayfield Road to take advantage of the steep drop. Hurtling down they went straight across the main road before racing down the slope and whizzing past the slaughter house door. If my mother had known about this she would have put an instant stop to it, because it was dangerous. There was more traffic about now than when we had done this. The speed these youngsters reached as they approached this busy road made it impossible for them to stop if anything was in their way.

Another noticeable difference was that the girls were more involved in the rough and tumble games than our girls had been, including taking their turn at driving in the Slaughter House Grand Prix. Ron, I know, kept a very strict eye on Jean whenever she was driving his cart.

For us these days were over; gone were our carefree racing games around the back cuts and boating on the river Itchen, although we still swam there. We went out in the evenings to more grown-up pursuits. Most of the gang looked the part and could get into the cinema if an X-rated film was showing, the age for this being sixteen. Even though I was now in long trousers, I still looked so young and needed to be in the middle of the group, out of the way of the cashier, to stand any chance.

Most of us had started smoking because it was considered a manly thing to do. Our fathers did this and we were eager to emulate them. We could buy five Woodbines from the little shops that adjoined our two favourite cinemas, the Savoy and the Palladium, and get away with saying they were for our fathers. This would not have worked in either of the two sweetshops of our younger days – Bailie's and Whitlock's – because we were so well known. Knowing our true ages they would have informed our parents we were trying to buy cigarettes.

We lived in better surroundings than most of our friends but, until now, I hadn't realised the full extent of this. The rules in each house were strictly laid down, and one of these was that bedrooms were for sleeping and nothing else. So once we came downstairs in the morning, the only times we were allowed back up during the day was when we needed something, like a change of clothes. Even though we went in and out of each other's houses on a regular basis, none of us ever went up to our friend's bedroom.

So on one of the days I called for Edwin Whelan he told me he had to take a bath before going out. That was alright with me, I could wait downstairs while he went up to the bathroom. I was shocked however when he said to me, 'No, I need your help with the bath.' What on earth was he talking about? My brother and I had been bathing ourselves for at least the past four years. It was all so simple so why on earth did Edwin need my help?

He explained that he needed to bring the tin bath in from the garden where it hung on the back wall. Once in the kitchen it would be filled with hot water from the copper. When finished with, the bath had to be lifted, one person at each end, and taken out to be emptied down the outside drain. Not an easy thing to do with water slopping about all over the place.

After going through this routine, and it was quite a struggle, I asked him the obvious question,. 'Why go through all this? What's wrong with using the bathroom?' He looked at me as though I had gone mad, 'What bathroom?'

'What do you mean what bathroom? The one upstairs of course,' I replied

'I don't know what you're talking about,' he said 'we haven't got a bathroom, and neither has anyone else, everyone bathes like this don't they?'

When I described our bathroom to him he obviously didn't believe me, so I invited him over to my house. Then with my mother's permission – after explaining the reason for it – we were allowed upstairs as far as the bathroom, where he stood and stared in awe. I showed him the geyser and explained how it worked to provide the hot water for the bath and how easy bath night was for us.

When news of this got out we were again referred to as the well-off family, because it was unusual for anyone to have anything as luxurious as a bathroom. The tin bath was used by almost every home in the country and, even though I had seen them hanging up in back gardens, I had no idea my friends had to go through this filling and emptying routine. It only came to light that day Edwin asked me to help him.

Ironically the prefabs, put up as temporary homes, did have an indoor bathroom, giving their occupants a distinct advantage over people whose homes had not been destroyed by Nazi bombing. My grandfather got used to this in the prefab he shared with gran until her death, when he moved in and lived with us for a while. He had been shown how to light the pilot light, swing it under the geyser to light the gas ring underneath, then turn on the water and wait for the bath to fill. This had to be done quickly because once the gas was turned on it came out of the main gas ring as well as the pilot tap, so speed was necessary to stop any build up.

Granddad announced one day that he wanted to take a bath and went upstairs. No-one thought anything about this until some fifteen to twenty minutes later, when we were all alerted by a huge bang. Rushing up we found him with his

clothes in tatters. Only his long johns were still intact, his hair was singed and standing on end, and his right arm was still outstretched towards the pilot light gas tap.
He had a spent match in his fingers and a look of total shock on his face.

He had turned the gas on and been unable to get a match to strike, some of them
must have been damp. When he did eventually succeed, an explosion was set off
from the accumulated gas. Fortunately he wasn't hurt, just severely shocked, and
nothing would get him to go in that room again. There was some structural damage
but one of the advantages of a father in the building trade was that he was able to
carry out the repairs himself.

My brother and two sisters were going out regularly each week to dances, but
I was still too young. Girls were beginning to loom larger and larger in all the
boys' lives. They weren't just mates anymore; we were now feeling much stronger
urges towards them as our sexual awareness progressed. I now knew why Vickie's
presence had always excited me, and the other girls we played with as children we
looked at completely differently. Edwin's sister, Sylvia, had joined in so many of our
childhood games, but now I saw her as the lovely young girl she had become. Tall,
with a slim figure, she too excited me whenever she came into the room.

We were shackled to a large extent by our upbringing, but most of us forged
ahead and got over this obstacle. Bobbie Westmore, Dave Simmonds, John Bates,
Edwin Whelan, the Priestly boys, and of course the irrepressible Pat Marriot, all had
a keen eye for the girls. Although it would still be a year or two before they put this
into practice, they were nonetheless well on their way.

As for me I suffered nothing but frustration. Skinny and young-looking, I thought
for a long time there was something wrong with me. I remember well going to the
fair with my school friends Michael Dibben and Malcolm Tizzard. All of us were
fourteen and met up with three girls the same age. Malcolm and Michael got dates
with two of them but the third was left with me and showed no interest at all. This
girl must have thought one of the other boys had brought their younger brother
along. There were however very strict rules about boy and girl behaviour. We had
heard stories of what went on in the back row of the cinema but this didn't come
to fruition. When our boys did make it to the back seat, it was a major achievement
if they even managed to put their arms around the girl's shoulders. Kissing and
touching were certainly tried, but were very rarely successful.

In the Spring of 1954 my sister, Pat, married Dan Higgs, and it took me some
time to realise the man we admired, so much – as he went careering around the
cycle track winning races for the Hawks Speedway team – was now my brother-
in-law. But he was, and in the late summer of 1955 he met me at the bottom of our
stairs with the words, 'Morning Uncle.' He and Pat were living in the front room
then, and by this he was telling me that she had given birth to their first-born son. I
felt really weird going to school that day and telling my class mates this news. It was
quite something to become an uncle while still only fourteen.

Our friend, and fellow Belgrave gang member, Andrew Selby, had been keeping us up-to-date about life with his eldest sister, Diana. For ten years none of the boys had ever called for Andrew at his home. If we did, and Diana opened the door, we would have been subjected to her sneering remarks, and if she could get close enough she would try to lash out with her fists.

Now though this had changed. Diana Selby, along with her friend Sally Farlow from Broadlands Road, had discovered the delights of boys for other reasons. A lot of the time these two wayward girls would sneak off down to the small arched bridge that carried the railway line over Kent road. Known to us all as the black arch, they weren't there to watch the trains but to meet local teenage boys from the surrounding roads.

It was always dark at night, an ideal spot for teenagers to meet in relative privacy. Nothing untoward happened beyond kissing, and what by today's standards would be regarded as mild flirting. But it was still not the way young ladies were expected to behave. Every night these two disappeared down the road coming back later and later, and it was Mr Selby who would be waiting at the front gate. Punishment would be swift; there was always the threat of the neighbours finding out if anything even remotely different occurred. Everyone was always afraid of this question, 'What will the neighbours say?'

Diana and Sally were looked upon with distaste by most of the female residents of Belgrave Road, even though Sally didn't live here. The dust finally settled on this affair when the Selby family announced the coming marriage of their eldest daughter to a local boy, Graham Pink. This was a boy she had met through Sally, as he too came from Broadlands Road. Now they could hold their heads up in public; their daughter was to become a respectable lady and all would be well with the world.

Things though do not always go to plan. The marriage went ahead and, after a full-white wedding, the two of them settled to married life in the front room of the Selby house. It lasted just under a year, when Graham, who couldn't stand life with Diana any more, packed up and went back to his family home. Her dislike of the male sex was still deep-rooted, and while she might like meeting boys and flirting with them, it was a different thing altogether when she had to live with one. She did try again and over a number of years married at least six times, but not one of those marriages lasted more than a few years.

She did surprise me one day though just after she became Mrs Pink. I was outside the Selby house talking to Andrew when the door opened and Diana came out. She actually started to talk to us and it was the first time I had experienced this. She asked what I was planning to do with the rest of my life now that I was nearly at school-leaving age. I proudly told her my father was going to help me get an apprenticeship as a carpenter. She thought this over for a few minutes. 'Yes that's a good trade, but why don't you go away to sea? You'll be made if you do because all the girls love a sailor. You'll have the time of your life.' I took no notice of this advice at the time but it became significant a year later.

My eldest sister, Sue, married for the first time the same year as Diana Selby and hers didn't last long either. Over the next four decades she married again, more than once, producing four children along the way, three boys and one very remarkable girl. Remarkable because, after the third of her boys was born, she took medical advice and was sterilized, but this failed and she became pregnant again. She was told to terminate the pregnancy, because her own health was in jeopardy. She could even die if she attempted to have this baby. But Sue was made of sterner stuff and, in August 1967, her daughter Karen was born and is now a fully-grown woman with children of her own. We are all very proud of Sue for this.

I looked forward to going with my father to start life as an apprentice carpenter. With this in mind I started to look once again at this man who had come so suddenly into my life when I was just four and a half years old. In all the time since then he had never really spoken to any of us. He was either out working all hours or enjoying a pint of beer in the Brook Inn. If he did speak it was never on any subject except work. He certainly never said a word to anyone about his experiences in the Second World War. I looked at him with renewed vigour and started on a quest to answer that question asked by so many youngsters then; which was simply, 'What did you do in the war Daddy?'

It took far longer than I expected to shed any light on this vexing question. I didn't really gain much information until after my father's death in 1986. As he had such a bad time during his army service, it was hardly mentioned once he became a civilian again. He did mellow slightly towards the end of his life and told Ron and Jean some of the things that happened while he was fighting for the country. Also taken into his confidence was my nephew, Nicholas, Pat's youngest son, who became a proud Regimental Sergeant Major in the Parachute Regiment.

Volunteering for army service at the start of hostilities in 1939, he joined the Royal Army Service Corp. From there, until the start of 1944, he served in various roles, that of a lorry driver, sniper and dispatch rider. In those years many good friends were lost to enemy fire. He was never wounded himself, nonetheless, he saw so many of the men he either grew up with, or trained and served with, cut down before his eyes – these events caused him so much heartache.

He was involved in a boxing tournament at one stage and when it was his turn to fight found himself facing a huge man. The result of the fight, told in dad's own word, was that, 'He knocked me all around the bleeding ring, and I never even landed a bloody single punch on him.' After the tournament the two men became close friends.

Some two months later, during a break, while their regiment was advancing to engage the enemy, the two of them were playing cards. Suddenly there was a German attack and they dived together into the safety of a nearby ditch. Corporal

Marsh moved just a fraction of a second ahead of the giant. As they both landed in the ditch dad saw at once that a bullet had hit his buddy and killed him outright.

As his regiment continued to advance, dad reverted to the very dangerous job of motorcycle dispatch rider, in tandem with another of his close friends from before the war. This time, dad heard the shot from a German sniper's rifle and felt the bullet whiz past his face. His friend's motorcycle crashed and he lay sprawled on the ground with blood running from the fatal wound in his head. From here my father's patience snapped. How many more good friends and trusted colleagues were to fall in this way?

Feeling the need to hit back with more power, he volunteered for the most efficient and ruthlessly committed section of Britain's army. The commandos were the idea of Prime Minister Winston Churchill in June 1940, when Britain had her back to the wall and German forces occupied Europe. He ordered that special troops be trained for short, fast raids and sabotage – in enemy-held territory – to capture high-ranking officers and to destroy radar and communication stations.

For this, the men selected had to be tough, ruthless and very determined. They needed to be good swimmers and able to accept the fact they would be fighting much closer to the enemy than any of them had to date. It is one thing to fire at a soldier from a distance, but quite another to have to creep up behind him and kill him with the thrust of a knife, or strangle him with a garrotte. My father had grown-up in one of Southampton's tough neighbourhoods, Dukes Road in Bevois Valley. He grew up in conflict with the hard-cases of Portswood and Swaythling. A typical act, when any of these factions found themselves in the same place, was for a single individual from one camp to stand up and say, 'I'll fight the toughest man here.' The challenge was always accepted, resulting in a brutal fight in which one, and often both men were very badly hurt.

Swimming was done in the River Itchen at the St Denys' end. I swam here myself in later years, so I knew how dangerous this part of the river was, with a swift current that can catch out the unwary and sweep them downstream. More than once this resulted in loss of life. With these attributes behind him Corporal Marsh got through the selection interview and found himself in the highlands of Scotland. In front of him now was the toughest challenge of his life so far – to get through this training in order to gain the green beret of the British Commandos.

I have travelled the route from Southampton to Fort William and marvelled at the sights. These hills are magnificent to look at, rising above the Highland Railway line with streams cascading down their sides. Some of these go directly into the magnificent lochs while others rush along the foot of the hills in a raging torrent. Looking at these, I was transported back to my days with Edwin Whelan when we loved to build dams. To attempt that here would be impossible; our pathetic attempts would have been swept away in seconds, and if we got too close we would have suffered the same fate.

It was because of those mighty hills, mountains and sprawling glens that Scotland was chosen as a training centre, where my father came through and was assigned to Six Commando. He was a good cook and always carried utensils, so, whenever his unit stopped – in houses or by the roadside – he would take the opportunity to do a cook up, something the men around him were very appreciative of.

Once when his unit were pinned down under a savage and merciless mortar attack, they could do nothing but keep down and wait this out before moving on again. The orders were to move at first light. However, during this sustained bombardment, dad noticed that a lone Frenchman appeared to be standing guard over a large barn, oblivious to the danger all around him. Turning to his mate beside him he asked, 'What's that French bleeder doing standing there?'

Getting no answer to this query he determined to find out for himself. When the shelling eventually stopped, my father, in company with two others, made their way over to the now unguarded barn and forced their way in. The sight that met their eyes nearly knocked them off their feet. The barn was full to the rafters with vintage champagne. Taking a few moments to get over the shock, they gathered up as many cases of this as they could carry and returned to their unit. They did move, as ordered, at first light, but were, for the most part, still floating after the amount they had managed to consume in just less than two hours.

Moving forward he received permission to kill one of a herd of grazing cows. He soon discovered that a dead cow is very big and heavy, and impossible to move without considerable help. This he got from members of his troop as they used bayonets to cut up the carcass. Then, covered in blood, they actually managed to borrow a jeep to transport the meat to where they would be stopping for the night. A messy and laborious job, but Six Commando ate well that night.

During research for this book I was privileged to meet some of Six Commandos surviving members – men such as Bob Cubitt and Brian Stewart, who lives in Leicestershire and invited me to his home. Another commando who was present at the Elbe, though not in the D-Day landings, was Eric Oates and it was a pleasure to meet him and his wonderful wife. Eric was on a parachute course in England when that great flotilla set sail across the Channel on 6 June. I saw my father re-enact this scene in his mind during the mid-sixties when he watched the film, *The Longest Day*. Having put the war firmly behind him as soon as he returned home in 1945 he was now seeing a very authentic re-enactment of the commandos coming ashore under fierce fire on D-Day. From the expression of sheer emotion on his face, as he watched the screen, it was obvious he was remembering everyone who fell that day.

It is sad that after the war, in 1946, the commandos were disbanded, but they certainly would not be forgotten. Speaking to Brian Stewart and the rest, I have heard some very pertinent comments. Brian, for instance, went into the RAF and spent the rest of his working life with them, travelling around the world to various airfields, before settling down to retirement with his wife in the beautiful village where they now live.

Speaking to his wife in the pub where we had lunch, she told me when I got to her home I would see nothing that relates to the RAF, even though her husband spent so many years in that branch of the service. What I would see was a shrine to the commandos. I sat there surrounded by memories and listened to Brian telling me, with so much pride, of those days in the Second World War when he was part of this unique band of men.

Both Eric Oates and Bob Cubitt told me that, looking back on it all, they feel a sense of guilt that they killed so many German soldiers. I find this sad, but understandable. They were people who, under normal circumstances, would not intentionally harm another human being. The events of 1939-45 were not normal, but it was their sworn duty to kill enemy troops and run the appalling risk of being killed themselves.

In Fort William, on Sunday 12 November 2006, I had one of the proudest moments of my life, when, representing my father, I marched with these wonderful men, following a pipe band to the cenotaph in front of the Alexandria Hotel. There, standing to attention, I watched in silent admiration as wreaths were laid. Fort William is small but on that morning it was packed with spectators of all ages who come to see this each year. In the afternoon, by the side of the commando memorial at Spean Bridge in sight of Ben Nevis, I was once more moved, very near to tears, at the service of dedication to the British Commandos.

My father hardly ever mentioned his time with this elite core of men. He, like the rest of the men who made up the commandos, was a hero but all he would say in subsequent years when asked what he had done was, 'Me, I didn't do anything nipper, I just kept my head down.' In paying tribute to him now I know that statement is far from the truth and that he did his duty and fought so gallantly for this country.

From the men I have met and the stories they have told me I am proud to say I am the son of a commando. Many of these men are gone now, but they should never be forgotten. Their names should live on forever because of the things they did for the freedom of this country, against formidable enemies with a power-mad dictator at their head. Long live the commandos and God bless you all.

# 10

# A Life on the Ocean Waves

As 1956 began I left Portswood Secondary Modern and was starting out on a life of freedom. Now earning my own living and getting on with the business of becoming an adult, I still looked so young and could easily have passed as a twelve year old.

I had gone with my father, in November, to the offices of a building firm, to see about my prospects of getting an apprenticeship as a carpenter. They explained to dad that I would have to wait until I was sixteen. This meant I had a year to wait before I could do anything about it. Dad did enquire at other companies on my behalf, each time receiving the same answer.

So I started as a van boy working for a local laundry – not the one we had played by as children, but one at the other end of Belgrave Road. This was Amey's and its chimney was clearly visible. It was entered from Portswood Road, just past the Red Lion public house, and was the first of two jobs I did that year. I was particularly pleased when I saw children going to school knowing that I would never have to do this again. My job was a daily round, delivering clean laundry to a succession of customers, collecting money then picking up the dirty washing to take back.

Handling money was not difficult for me. I had done this many times while working for Ted Martin. I had also been taught mental arithmetic at school, as well as honesty from my mother. The day I received my first pay packet I felt 10ft tall. I opened the small brown envelope with my name written on it, and found the enormous amount of £3 10s. I gave £2 to my mother for my keep, and had the luxury of £1 10s for myself. I was a man of means. Thirty shillings would carry me effortlessly through the next week, allowing for lunches in the work's canteen and trips to the cinema at least twice a week.

When Edwin Whelan suggested we go to Southampton's stadium, where our speedway team performed on a weekly basis, I was only too pleased to comply. He told me about the greyhound racing that took place every Saturday evening. Entering the stadium we were both caught up in the excitement and atmosphere of a meeting, from the track to the many bookmakers and the general noise of the place. We were going to bet on the tote so followed the other men around to the small windows and listened. Placing a bet on the first two dogs past the post, regardless of the order in which they finished, seemed the best way to do it. It wasn't the best of starts, as the two we picked came fourth and last.

'We should have bet on the hare,' Eddy said as we threw away our betting slip. We were no more successful in the next race, but the third one we watched in such excitement as our two dogs raced to the front and crossed the line almost together. We broke a few speed records ourselves as we went around to the tote to collect our winnings.

We did it again in the fifth and sixth races and left the stadium with more money than either of us had before we went in. Wow I thought, if money is as easy as this to come by then we must do it every week. I saw such a rosy future. Just pick the right dogs and you're in clover, money for old rope was firmly in my mind.

So the very next Saturday luck was really on our side, because we ran into one of the men who lived in Belgrave Road.

'Hey,' he said, 'what are you two doing here?' We told him it was our second time, and that we had won money last Saturday. 'Ok boys, stick with me tonight, I'll see you're alright.'

We did just that and bet on each selection he told us, but lost every time. As we left the stadium I realised with a shock that I had bet and lost all my money on those dogs. I now had a whole week ahead of me and had nothing. It was a harsh lesson, but one very definitely learned. Neither of us went greyhound racing again; I never gambled again after that night.

I would have spent all year at the laundry had it not been for a conversation I had with Dave Simmonds at the end of April. He and Bobbie Westmore were working in the saw mill of a timber company in Southampton Docks. They were looking for more staff and he suggested I come and join them. Pat Marriott also came to work here when he left school that summer, so now four Belgrave boys were working together.

We had our own bikes by now – proper ones with chains, tyres and saddles – and cycled to work, entering through dock gate No. 10. Having set my sights on becoming a carpenter I should have been in my element here, working with wood. In the confines of the saw mill I was always kept busy, either on one of the lathes or the circular saws.

During lunch breaks we went into the small canteen where we could eat our sandwiches and enjoy a hot drink. From here I could see over to the shipping berths where a liner from Union Castle was always visible. There were cargo ships as well as those from other lines, notably Cunard, P&O and Royal Mail. As I gazed at these I remembered the advice given to me by Diana Selby. She had painted a picture of travel, coupled with the admiration and availability of girls, and her words echoed inside my head.

Edwin Whelan had always fantasised about ships. He had books and talked endlessly about them. We had gone year by year to the dockyards at Portsmouth for the Royal Navy open days where I trailed after him onto one warship after another. We all thought he would go away to sea at the first possible chance, either in the Royal or Merchant Navy. Edwin, however, had other ideas and went straight to British Railways where he became an apprentice boilermaker, and worked at this trade in the Eastleigh Railway yards for many years.

I gazed at these elegant ships, and within me came a longing to be on board; and to travel to various parts of the world. Week after week this urge became more pronounced, until I plucked up the courage to once again approach my father. There was no easy way to put this because dad had already done a lot to put me in line for an apprenticeship as a carpenter. So I just came out with it and explained to him that I had changed my mind and would now like to join the Merchant Navy. He looked keenly at me, 'Have you thought this out properly?' I told him I was sure this was something I really wanted to do, 'Righto nipper, leave it to me,' he replied.

A few weeks later I received a letter from the headquarters of the British Merchant Marine. This invited me to present myself at the offices of the Shipping Federation, situated at Terminus Terrace, alongside Terminus railway station. The boat trains from London came through here bringing passengers for all the major liners, including the *Titanic* back in 1912.

I had to be there at ten in the morning for a medical. I got the necessary time off from the timber yard and rode my bike the short distance. I almost changed my mind as I got my first sight of this imposing building. To say it was Victorian doesn't even come close. It was a dark and gloomy looking place and on the ground floor was a long counter where seamen came in search of berths on various ships. I, however, was directed upstairs to see the doctor.

The medical examination was very tough, and there was concern about my small stature. I was still short, boyish-looking and decidedly skinny. But there was nothing wrong with my health, and, as the end of the year came in sight, I received another letter. This one told me I had been given a place at the National Sea Training School at Sharpness in Gloucestershire, commencing in February 1957. At this I was over the moon and I thanked my father for his help in getting me there. Then at the end of January I handed in my notice at the timber yard and prepared to start on the great adventure that was now beckoning me.

The day I set out for this was daunting to say the least. I was just sixteen years old and up until this moment had never been away from home. Our parents had their work cut out just providing food and clothing as well as the rent and household bills. So holidays for the Marsh family, and everyone else in the road, were out of the question. We had occasionally gone away for day trips, but until now I had never slept anywhere but in the bedroom overlooking the railway line in Belgrave Road. Now I was heading for a course lasting six weeks, and would be sleeping in a dormitory with lots of other boys from all over the country.

With some trepidation I stood with other members of my family on the platform of Southampton Central Station, in the first week of February 1957. As the train pulled out I waved wildly to them until they were out of sight then settled back on the seat as the train gathered speed.

I was surprised when another boy, who I hadn't even noticed and was in the same compartment, suddenly spoke. 'Excuse me, but are you by any chance going to the sea school in Sharpness?' I of course told him I was and it was a comfort to have someone from my own town travelling with me. We hit it off from the start and all the way up to Bristol, where we had to change trains. He told me just what was laying ahead for us both.

He had friends already at sea that had gone through the same training course. The tales he told of the hardship ahead were harrowing, but any time during the first three weeks of the course you could quit and go home if you couldn't take it. When he said this he was looking keenly at me and making the same mistake so many others had before him; because I was small and skinny he obviously thought I was weak as well.

I was partly dressed in the latest craze, that of a Teddy boy. I didn't have the knee-length jacket I normally wore – this had been left at home – but I did have my black drain-pipe trousers. These were well named as it was necessary to bend your feet as far forward as they would go in order to pull them on, where they clung to your legs just like a second skin.

In my suitcase were four white shirts with no collars attached. My father still wore shirts like these and had to have them starched. These stiff collars had to be secured by studs, one at the back and two in front. I had watched dad doing this on so many occasions and was always glad the shirts we wore weren't like this. This ordeal was before me now though, as these shirts had to be worn with the blue serge uniform that the sea school supplied. I had the Teddy boy haircut called a Tony Curtis, with a front quiff named after the Hollywood film star, and what was called a, 'DA', at the back. For me this was just the latest thing to wear but some of the hard-cases, of the day, had gone way too far.

The jackets for instance had large velvet lapels, and some unscrupulous boys had sewn full length razor blades inside them. So anyone starting a fight and grabbing hold of both lapels would find their hands very badly cut. I was never in this league, fighting was something I only did when I couldn't possibly avoid it, so I was a Teddy boy in looks only. But this didn't mean I was as weak as my new companion obviously thought.

A little train carried us from Bristol, across the viaduct over the River Severn, to the quaint little station at Sharpness. Getting off we found ourselves amongst nearly thirty boys, most of whom were dressed in the same Teddy-boy style. Every one of them looked at me and formed the same opinion. I was nominated right there and then as the first boy to go running home to mother.

My first sight of the camp left me wondering what I had got myself into. We were all signed in, then taken to the hut that would be our home for the next three weeks. There were three of these allocated to the boys taking the catering course, and the squad I was in were shown to hut B3. Like the other two, it had double-tiered bunks running down both sides of a long and extremely cold room, which had only one stove. This was in the centre and did little to raise the temperature above the extreme cold outside.

We were told to find ourselves a bunk and dump our suitcases on it. I took a lower bunk halfway down, as near to the stove as I could get. Then leaving my case I followed the rest back to the camp entrance. Here we were shown a small parade ground. There were two of these, the other was much larger and more important and was on the other side of the grounds. The recreation hall had a very large cinema-sized television screen so that large numbers of boys could watch TV together in the evenings. Then it was over to the washroom, called 'ablutions', to be shown where we could wash and keep our kit clean. In the gloom of that first night I failed to see how sparse this particular room was.

The training ship *Vindicatrix* was reached by a path from the camp that led to the Severn canal where she was permanently berthed. As we came in sight of her we had to endure taunts from a whole mass of Vindi boys ranged along the upper deck overlooking the gangway. 'Hey new boys, welcome to hell on earth, you ain't never gonna see your homes again new boys.'

Everyone had to go through this; it was a ritual meted out each Monday to let them know they were the juniors.

My first look at the *Vindicatrix* left me with a mix of dread and admiration. She had started life as a wonderful tall-masted ship, the *Aranmore*, but now didn't seem to be in one piece. This was because she no longer had any of the three masts that once stood proudly from her deck, nor the long bow sprit. These had been cut down once she was commissioned as a training ship in 1939.

We were taken down to the mess deck. Here at long tables the *Vindi* boys sat to eat the meagre meals that were served up three times a day. All new boys had to face a plate of Sea Pie. This was a mixture of corned beef and vegetables, cooked into what I can only describe as a mess. We were used to the lovely meals our mothers served up at home, and they bore no resemblance to this. The tea was served from metal jugs and this was unbelievable. Most of my squad simply couldn't eat this and it was pushed to one side. Here it was promptly snatched by boys from other squads who were hungry and knew that new boys, at least on their first experience of a Vindi meal, wouldn't be able to face it. By next morning, however, we were as hungry as any of them so nothing was left over from any other meal for the rest of our course.

Then it was over to the kit hut where uniforms and day-wear were issued. I was quite lucky here because the navy blue jacket, blue trousers and black socks actually fitted me quite well. Others were not so lucky and had uniforms that were either too big or too small. Also issued were off-white jackets to the boys taking the catering course, to be worn during the day inside the camp. They were known as pea jackets and resembled the white steward's jackets we would be required to wear on passenger ships at sea. We grew to hate these as they gave us the nickname of 'PJs'. Also issued were vests and black shorts for morning's physical training (PT).

Once this was taken back to our hut and put carefully away in the lockers and drawers, we had to sew Merchant Navy shoulder flashes onto the uniform jackets. I had never used a needle before and took absolutely ages trying to thread one. Amazingly we managed to complete this job before being left to ourselves for the rest of the evening. We spent this time wandering about, trying to find our way around this new and alien place, before our first night there. Then we had to get undressed and put on pyjamas, which was a first for me. Our parents had not been able to supply things like this. All of us, girls as well as boys, simply wore underwear in bed. The rules for this camp were that all boys would wear them, so I bought myself a pair out of sheer necessity.

Coming into the hut that first night I found one of the hardships was going to be understanding what my new companions were saying to me. There were boys from all parts of the country and they spoke in various accents. I couldn't understand them and they, to my total surprise, couldn't understand me. I didn't think I had a Hampshire accent at all; not having been out of my own county before I had only heard my native accent being spoken. Things got better as the weeks went by and we got to know each other, but that first day I thought I had come to a foreign country.

I got through roll-call, standing at the foot of our bunks, our bare feet touching the freezing floor. Shivering as I answered my name I now crawled into my hard and uncomfortable bunk. I then spent a very long night, a long way from home, in a room full of strangers. The next day was much worse. It started at half six in the morning with a bugle sounding, then the hut door crashing open and a voice yelling, 'Everyone up'.

There was no arguing with this. At home my mother had to call me at least three times before I left the warmth and comfort of my bed, but this was a direct order and none of us were left in any doubt. We fell out of our bunks, grabbed our wash things and went outside. It was so cold, I swear that even the icicles hanging down from the roofs of the huts had icicles on them.

We were marched over to ablutions for morning wash, and it is difficult to remember whether it was colder inside this hut than outside. Because of our young age, none of us had to worry about shaving, but washing in cold water was no joke at all. Once this ordeal was over we had to march to the small parade ground for PT.

This was a normal morning requirement in those first three weeks of the course. Standing in line, dressed sparsely in vests and shorts and shaking with the cold, we were glad when the officer in charge arrived. He had us running around the parade ground doing various exercises; it was hard but at least it warmed us up a bit. When this was over we had to double back to our hut and quickly make the bunks, then change into our everyday wear; black trousers, white shirt and pea jacket.

The *Vindicatrix* was imposing but also a grand sight. I have always been intrigued by tall ships and she was certainly one of these. Even though she was going nowhere she had all the attributes of her kind, including a figure head, a female carving known as Mrs Drysdale.

An accident had happened here only a few months ago where a boy had been very badly hurt. He was attempting to carry out a long held Vindi tradition – crawling out on what was left of the bow sprit to reach down and touch the figure head's left breast. This boy had leaned out too far and fallen, with the result being that the practice was outlawed. It was a tradition going back over a number of years, and was designed to show they had what it takes to become a Vindi boy. I was very glad this was no longer allowed, because I have absolutely no head for heights. That figure was a long way from the ground and I know I would have failed.

The Vindi was moored alongside a quay and had two gangplanks, one for boarding and the other for disembarking ,and she was surrounded by lifeboats. We on the catering course had to pass lifeboat training as well, although rowing in time with everyone else was something I never mastered. Before boarding we had to walk past the toilet block on the quayside. It was a small brick hut that backed onto the mighty River Severn and had a line of pans along one wall, and a row of sinks facing them. To say it was sparse goes nowhere near to describing this building. The toilet pans had neither seats nor cubicles, so privacy was nowhere to be seen and the smell in there was something every Vindi boy will remember.

Once aboard the ship, on that first day, we were taken again to the tween deck area. Here we had shock number two – namely breakfast. This time the meal we were given consisted of a cup of tea that tasted more like diesel oil and a plate of what we were told was porridge. How anyone could make this traditional breakfast cereal taste so bad will always remain a mystery to me. The only reason any of us actually ate it, was because, by then, we were very hungry indeed. So, despite the hopeful looks of the more senior boys around us, nobody left anything. The food we were given after this varied only in content, the taste was always terrible.

The classrooms were on a deck below. Here, over the next six weeks, we would learn everything members of the catering department of a merchant ship needed to know in order to do their jobs. We had to practice properly and get this right because we would have to do this for real soon and wait on the ship's officers and captain.

We needed to learn how to look after ourselves as well. Up until now clothes were taken off and simply thrown in the wash basket ready for mum. The next time we saw them they were washed, ironed and ready to wear again. Here there was only one person who would look after our laundry requirements and that was ourselves. We had instruction in the proper way to hand wash everything, in cold water and with hard carbolic soap, and then iron and fold clothes so they would always be not only clean but smart as well.

On the first Sunday the camp inmates had to line up on the main parade ground for captain's inspection. The uniforms had to be faultless and the trousers pressed to perfection, with creases you could cut your finger on. Clean and freshly ironed shirts were also necessary, and we had to be spotless with clean nails and hair smartly combed. So in that first week this was drummed into us very thoroughly indeed.

I found out how important it is to have allies, preferably ones who were bigger than you. I had this advantage while growing up in Belgrave Road and during my time at school. Help was always on hand whenever I was facing trouble I couldn't handle myself. Here though I was on my own, easily the smallest boy in my squad and therefore fair game for the rest of the lads.

This came home to me on the third morning. I changed from my PT gear and had on my daytime uniform, but failed to notice a small knot of boys standing together just inside the door. As I reached them they pounced on me, pinning me to the deck. My jacket and trousers were pulled off and I was dragged outside. Then they all ran off, taking my trousers with them. I was left to walk down to the ship like this, looking for my clothes, which I eventually found tied to the path fence.

When I arrived on board I was already late and my explanation of being held up in the ablutions was grudgingly accepted. But I missed breakfast, and on the *Vindi* that was a fate worse than death. The fact I had not said what actually happened gave me credibility and the experience hardened me considerably. From then on I never went anywhere alone and always gave groups of boys a wide berth.

I found out quickly who I could rely on and realised that two of my squad were very close indeed. These were the boy in the bunk above me whose name was Terry Forman, and in the lower bunk, next to me, was the dependable and large form of Ron Woodford. We three formed a friendship that was good for us all and for the rest of our course we went everywhere together. In the evenings most of the inmates walked the short distance to Sharpness Docks. This certainly included the three of us who were now recognised and called the terrible three.

In this area we could find both the dockside café and the missions to seamen. Both these places gave us the thing all Vindi boys desperately needed, which was food. We could get mugs of real tasting tea for 6d as well as buns or sandwiches; and in the mission, hot buttered toast. This was not too much of a demand on the 5s a week pocket money we were allowed, and it was heaven for us all after the food we were expected to eat in camp.

There was entertainment of sorts here from a man known to us, and a very long line of Vindi boys before, simply as Mark. He had met our train as it came into Sharpness station, as he did every week, greeting each new intake with the words, 'I'm Mark. I meet all the new Vindi boys.' He was very friendly, played the piano and said our time here would go so fast we wouldn't even notice the six weeks passing. None of us believed this of course, but just being here, out of camp, was enough.

The problem was that to 'go ashore', or in other words leave the confines of the camp, it was necessary to wear uniform. This in turn meant wearing crisp white shirts with the starched collars. The first time I tried to fasten these was a nightmare. The back stud was easy to put in, it could be done before the shirt was pulled over the head. Then the collar was fastened, the black tie being inserted inside it first. So far so good, but now the front stud was put into place and held the top of the shirt together, while both sides of the collar were pulled round and fastened to it, one on top of the other. This had to be done while holding the tie in place as well.

Fixing these two sides of the collar to the front stud was something I found nearly impossible; more than once either Terry or Bob, fed up with waiting for me and watching this nightly struggle, stepped in and did it for me, much to my relief. Ron Woodford in particular told me I needed to start growing.

'Your too much of a titch for this, your fingers are too small for the studs.'

Many boys experienced the harsh discipline. Breaking into the camp's bread locker for some much needed extra food was a common occurrence, and saw the boy (or boys) responsible being told to report under the clock. The dreaded punishment order meant the offenders would be given 'jankers'. This meant being confined to camp and given menial jobs to do in the evenings. The confinement was far worse than the boring jobs meted out.

Some of the boys walked to Berkely village, a few miles up the road from Sharpness, to go to the cinema there. I even heard tales of Vindi boys getting a train across the Severn viaduct and going into Lydney. The terrible three – myself, Terry and Ron – never did this because of the time it took. We had to be back in camp on time every night if we wanted to go out again the next evening, so all three of us made sure we never missed roll-call.

There was another embarrassing episode that first week, and this happened on our fourth day. We had turned up for morning PT to find our officer instructor was late. We were kept waiting for at least ten minutes and were extremely cold by the time he eventually arrived, so cold in fact that our knees had started to knock together. He looked terrible, unshaved and bleary eyed, as he stood and glared. Then he roared at us saying, he had never seen a group of boys in such a filthy state before, and ordered us off his parade ground.

'Go and have a bath at once,' he roared. This was totally unjustified because compared to him we were immaculate.

In all the time we had been here I didn't even know we had baths. We were sent back for wash things then told to make our way over to the camp ablutions. For the second time that morning we had to strip completely. When we had done this we joined a queue of boys who were as naked as we were, and waited our turn at one of the sinks.

Everything I had so far been taught about life was being challenged. My mother had drummed into us that certain parts of our bodies were private, and were always to be kept that way. During my childhood no-one, not even the members of the Belgrave gang, had seen me in anything less than underwear. Now I was standing completely naked in a long queue of boys, all in the same state of complete undress. I was shivering with a mixture of cold and embarrassment as we shuffled forward.

When it was our turn at the sinks we had to wash all over then rinse off the soap with freezing cold water. If that was not enough we had to do it all again and there was a boson at the head of each line to make sure each boy did this properly. When at last this dreadful experience was over, it was double back to the hut, and thankfully into day uniform. Bath night at No.94 Belgrave Road was never anything like this.

We were in the hut for the first three weeks of our course and started to mock the new boys every week. From the deck of the Vindi we could see right over to the railway viaduct and eagerly watched the sugar-puff train, which looked just like the one used to illustrate packets of puffed wheat, as it chugged over. We looked down on these new boys from here and let them know we were halfway through our course, whereas theirs was just starting.

As that third week was coming to a close, and we would be moving from the camp to live aboard the *Vindi*, there were two very notable things that took place. The first of these was a lecture that had to be attended by all the boys, so shore leave was cancelled that night. This was so we could meet in the main recreation hall to learn all about the dangers of sex. Most of us up until then hardly knew anything about the pleasures of sex, let alone the dangers. But we were training for a career that would take us to many parts of the world, and women would play a big part in this.

This lecture was about syphilis and gonorrhoea. The lecturer was a little man who really knew his subject and he frightened the life out of us with his descriptions of these terrible diseases. At the end of this ordeal not one boy who heard it, and saw the dreadful pictures of what happens to the male body, would ever have wanted to have sex with any woman anywhere.

It was at the end of the lecture that the professor completely lost the plot. For over an hour he had frightened us to death, now he told us these things were treatable if discovered in time. The way to find out if you have contracted either one of these was simple. 'Grasp your testicles in the palm of your hand and gently squeeze; if you have a sharp pain as a result of this action you must see the Medical Officer immediately.'

This was greeted with a stunned silence, followed almost immediately by uproarious laughter. Frightened we may have been but this was hilarious. There were calls from all over the hall about squeezing that particular part of the body, and while this was going on the professor was trying to regain control. His squeaky voice appealed to us, 'Really gentlemen I'm quite serious about this.' But the more he appealed the louder we got until eventually one of our own officers came up onto the stage and roared for silence.

That was the end of the lecture but I for one have never forgotten it. As far as sex was concerned, a lot of the Vindi boys were more advanced than I was. But even these lotharios never had any success with the local girls in Sharpness. This was due, undoubtedly, to the nightly cocoa, which unknown to us was laced with bromide. This considerably dampened our sex drive and was available to us every night, on a drink as much as you like basis. The result was that we lost any interest, and as the local girls knew this they didn't come anywhere near us.

The second notable thing to take place happened on the last but one day that my squad spent in the huts. We were destined to move down onto the *Vindi*. Here we would live in one of the below-deck dormitories for the last weeks of the course. Our numbers had been considerably reduced by this time. A lot of the boys, mostly the hard-cases, found that physical strength alone was not enough to get through. The discipline, the awful food and having to do everything yourself was too much for them.

We needed inner strength and the determination to win through. The *Vindi* turned boys into men and the course was made as tough as this to test everyone. If you couldn't take what she threw at you then you weren't cut out for a life at sea. At least a dozen boys who had arrived to start their course at the same time as me, and who had predicted that I would be the first one to leave, had themselves gone running home to mother. I was delighted I was still here and was now determined that nothing was going to stand in my way of completing the course.

We had all gone out to the missions to seaman in the village which was somewhat different from when we arrived three weeks ago. Mark had been there every night with his piano-playing and advice. He had been doing this for years and he had entertained many Vindi boys. Now though, the mission had taken advantage of an offer from some of the village girls to come and be there as well.

We were delighted when this happened, but Mark took offence, to the tune of giving an ultimatum. He told the manager to either get rid of the girls, or he would go. All the Vindi boys were then asked to vote. The result was overwhelming; we may not have been thinking of sex, but we still automatically enjoyed the company of girls. I believe this situation was resolved and he did return to his nightly stints with the boys at the mission, but that was after we had finished our course and gone home.

On that last night of the camp huts we came back to find that our officer, who was due to take roll-call, was ill. This meant that we, as well as the two squads behind us, had to go over to the main parade ground where one of the deck officers was waiting to step in. All the boys who were training to be deck hands considered themselves tougher than us in the catering department. Their course was ten weeks compared to our six. We of course disputed this – we were as tough as any one of them – and on this night we thought we would prove it.

As we all lined up on the parade ground, the officer who stepped forward was the most feared man in the whole camp. Small in stature he was none-the-less the most disciplined officer. All the boys under his command both respected and feared him, and not one of them ever did anything to upset this particular man. His real name I can't even remember because he was known to us all by the nickname of 'Popeye'. This was said behind his back of course, never to his face. We had heard stories about him and were understandably nervous. He stood in front of us glowering. He had a way of looking straight at you and making you squirm, before starting on the roll-call. When answering roll-call each boy either said 'Yes Sir' or 'Here Sir.'

Suddenly from one of the back ranks a loud voice shouted 'Pop Pop'; one of the new boys was trying to be funny, he hadn't said the whole of the nickname, but the inference was clear. Popeye stopped calling names and all of us held our breath. We couldn't believe someone had dared to do something like this and waited for his reaction. 'Who's the funny man?', he asked. Needless to say there was no answer so he repeated the question, 'I'll ask just one more time, who's the funny man?'

When there was still no answer he went on with the roll-call and then dismissed us. We were astounded; the mighty and fearful Popeye had been laughed at by one of our boys and we got away with it. The deckies must really be wimps if they were scared of this lightweight. We were still laughing as we undressed and got into our bunks. The lights were turned out and peace descended on the hut.

One hour later this was severely and very rudely shattered. The hut door burst open and we were ordered to get up and dressed in our uniforms. For me this meant the usual struggle with the collar studs and now I was having trouble just keeping my eyes open. So I cheated and used the tie to cover the fact that neither of the front parts of the collar were secured to the stud. I could get away with this in the dark, but not at any other time.

Once dressed, we were marched over to the main parade ground where Popeye was waiting for us. Lining up he said those words that were going to give us nightmares before the end of the night. 'Who's the funny man?'

Still getting no reply we were marched back again made to undress properly then get into pyjamas before turning in to our bunks. That was without any doubt the toughest night of my course. Every hour, on the hour, it was get up, get dressed and get over to the parade ground to be asked who the funny man was. We somehow got through it and all of us now knew why this officer was so feared.

We never gave the culprit away, but by lunchtime the next day we knew who had been the cause of our nightmare. By then the boy concerned had owned up, either by his own realisation of the trouble he had caused to so many other boys or by succumbing to the persuasion of the rest of his squad. Popeye proved he was not only tough but shrewd, he knew that by punishing everyone he would get to know who had dared to openly insult him. The guilty boy got jankers which confined him to camp for the next week, as well as a lot of very embarrassing punishments meted out to him by the rest of his squad.

The first three weeks had dragged but now the time was quite literally whizzing past. We had moved from the huts and were settled in our dormitory on board the *Vindi*, where the terrible three all landed plumb jobs. Ron Woodford had come out best as he was made Captain's Tiger. This meant he was the Camp Captain's personal steward and spent most of his days in the house Captain Poor shared with his attractive daughter. It also meant Ron had special privileges within the camp. I pointed this out to him one night when he joined the rest of us for inspection at the gate before being allowed out for the evening.

'You don't have to do this Ron,' I hissed at him and realising this was true he simply walked past the officer on duty and out through the gate. Unfortunately this officer saw it was me who gave Ron that piece of information and the glare he gave me quite clearly said, 'I saw that so you'd better watch yourself from now on.'

As for Terry Foreman and I, we were cook's stewards and we had perks too. Our own little mess was at the back of the galley and from here we got the same wonderful food that was served to the officers. This to a Vindi boy was the equivalent of winning the football pools and made up for so much.

When it was Terry's turn to get the food, he came into the mess and I thought he had spilled meat stew all over the rice pudding. When I pointed this out and asked how we were supposed to eat this he simply laughed at me. 'Haven't you ever had curry? It's supposed to be served like this.'

I was still very doubtful because I had never eaten rice as a vegetable before. Mum always served it up with milk after it had been cooking so that it had a lovely brown skin on top, and was sweet. So I argued this with Terry who was most unsympathetic. He got two helpings of dinner that day, because it would be many years before I could actually enjoy curry and rice.

At no time did I feel homesick. Considering this was the first time in my life I had lived anywhere but Belgrave Road, surrounded by all of the really wonderful friends I grew up with, I should have felt lost and lonely. The course was so tough that like everyone else I spent each day simply concentrating on survival. So I never even thought of home at all.

At the end of the fifth week we all had to report to the camp nurse for a medical, to see how we had fared since our arrival. The nurse was a very large lady, her name was Sister Gray, but she was known to us all as 'Codeine Annie'. The nickname was earned because this was her stock answer to everything medical. No matter what was wrong with you, if you had to see her she always gave codeine as a remedy.

However, if anyone was really ill they were taken into the infirmary where proper medical attention could be administered.

When it was my turn for the check up I was alarmed when she announced I was under the weight I had been five weeks ago when I started the course. This, coupled with the fact I was small and in her opinion sickly looking, was why she told the officer on duty I should be admitted to the infirmary. There she could keep an eye on me for the next few days. I was acutely aware that like the rest of my squad I was just one week away from completing the course and heading back. Three days in the infirmary would mean I would lose the best part of a week's training; this in turn would mean a week added to my course.

I was having none of this. I may have had a plumb job with much better food, but I was eager to get this finished and leave the *Vindi* behind me. I pleaded my case so firmly that I convinced the medical officer, and eventually Codeine Annie, herself, that I had never felt better in my life. I was underweight, but that was because the food served up in the first three weeks was so bad and there was very little of it.

I survived the medical, passed the final exam then woke up on the final morning of the course. After breakfast we went to see the chief steward to receive our seaman's discharge books. All of these had a copy of a photograph we had posed for two days before. Sitting in front of a camera in our Vindi uniforms, we had a picture taken with our discharge number on a plank held across our chest; it served the same purpose as a passport photo. Our fingerprints were taken and these were displayed on the inside of the discharge books. I thought these made us look more like convicts than seaman, but it meant we had done it. We had survived the course and could now go to sea.

It was with such pride that I accepted mine, along with the chief steward's congratulations on passing the course and best wishes in our future careers in the Merchant Navy. It had been the hardest six weeks of my life – there were times when I didn't even know how to cope, but just had to knuckle down and carry on. In some cases though, especially boys coming here from homes that were really bad, the *Vindi* seemed like a four-star hotel. One of these came from a very large family and always had to share a bed with at least three of his brothers. Coming to the *Vindi* was the first time in his life he had slept in a bed on his own.

For most of us though it had been hell on earth, so it was with mounting excitement that we all went to the gate carrying our suitcases, and in our best uniforms, to be finally discharged. We passed captain's inspection and all of us knew that if anything was found to be wrong with our uniforms, the unfortunate boy would fall out and report under the clock where a week would be added to his course. My squad was determined this terrible fate would not happen to any of us. We had come this far together and would all be going home the same way. So we inspected each other before to make absolutely sure we would pass.

The last order we received as we walked out the main gate to walk to the station was, 'Don't run.' No chance; as soon as we were out of sight of the camp there was a stampede to the station and the hated berets we always had to wear with the Vindi uniforms were snatched from our heads and thrown into the air. Some boys were so pleased to be going home to decent food and comfort ,they took off their uniforms, and threw them out of the train windows.

How well I remember sitting on the train, being pulled by the little sugar puff engine, gazing across for my last look at the *Vindi* as we crossed the Severn Railway Viaduct on our way into Lydney. How many times had I stood on the *Vindi*'s deck and watched this train going back and forth across here, and counted the time in hours, days, and weeks, when at last I would be on it with the course behind me. Now it was happening, and as we travelled home the same boy who had been with me on our way here, told me told me how surprised he was that I had made it. 'We all thought you wouldn't last a week.' But I had – privately I was as surprised as everyone else.

Getting back into Southampton I was overjoyed and even more so when I once again entered Belgrave Road. Having not seen it for six weeks I realised then how much I had missed it. I came up the road in a taxi and told the driver just after he passed the bombed buildings to stop at the next lamp post on the right. I was to do this many times over the next few years when I came home.

My mother was delighted to see me again and I was surprised by the way she had missed me. I was the first of her six children to leave home for any reason at all. With a family this size she had always been so busy on a day-to-day basis looking after us that I didn't think I would be missed. But as soon as I walked through the familiar front door she threw her arms around me and all but crushed me in her embrace.

She told me she had been unable to accept that one of her children was no longer under her roof, and for most of the time I had been away she had automatically put out a plate for me when serving up the family meals, only to realise I wasn't there to eat it. Although this did get better over the next few years when I was away much more than I was at home, she still had a hard time coping with it. I spent two weeks just getting used to being home again and regaining the weight I had lost at sea school with a lot of my mother's cooking. But then it was time to report once again to the Shipping Federation offices to be assigned to my first ship.

# 11

# Sea Air and Cape Brandy

The first thing I had to do was report to the Southampton branch of the missions to seamen, also situated in the dock area, to meet the chaplin. He did the same for me as he did for everyone just starting out and gave me a Bible. Although I wasn't anywhere near as religious as my mother, that Bible meant a lot to me and I had it with me everywhere I went.

My first ship was a tanker; they needed a galley boy and I got the berth. She was a coaster so I wouldn't be going overseas. But after serving for just a few weeks I gained a liking for these particular ships. Her name was the *Esso Apalachee*, part of a fleet of tankers named after American Indian tribes.

When I first went to join her I had to get a ferry from Southampton's town quay. This was run exclusively for the crews of tankers berthed at Fawley oil refinery. Because it was my first ship, dad decided to accompany me – he could come on the ferry but would not be able to land as only ships crews were allowed. I was glad he was there though. Even though I had got through the course at sea school, going to join my first ship was a daunting prospect.

Arriving at Fawley I shook hands with my father, then mounted the steps leading up to the dockside. There before me was the towering shape of the *Esso Apalachee*. I was overawed as I approached the gangway and looked up at her, then went on deck and was met by the second steward. He would be my immediate boss and was himself answerable to the head of the catering department, the chief steward.

He welcomed me on board then showed me to the boy ratings cabin. All tankers carried three boys, two in the ships pantries and one in the galley. Having introduced me to my new shipmates I was left to unpack. The cabin was spacious with three bunks, one on the port side and two, top and bottom, on the starboard side. I was given the lower one with a locker and drawer for shirts and socks.

Then it was up to get my first ever look at a ship's galley. I was to be kept very busy here, getting vegetables from the store during the morning and preparing them ready for the ship's cook. After this, my day consisted largely of washing up the many saucepans and dishes. I learned how tight discipline is aboard a British ship, punctuality and cleanliness being of paramount importance. Although this ship did not go overseas it made no difference to the onboard routine. Sundays were captain's inspection and fingers were worked to the bone to make sure everything was spotless.

Although I was only a member of this ship's company for a few weeks, she certainly served a purpose. It was a gentle introduction to life in the Merchant Navy. I got to see a lot of the country of my birth as we carried oil in and out of Liverpool and Elsmere then back to Fawley, which meant I could get home and spend at least one night in my own bed before rejoining the next day. She was a comfortable ship, with good accommodation, good food and a friendly, happy crew.

The *Apalachee* served me in one other important way. She was a conventional tanker with a catwalk connecting the stern to the centre island. When these ships are fully loaded they lie so low that in any kind of sea, huge amounts of water crash over and anyone in the way can easily be swept over the side. The cat walk was necessary for safety.

The waters around Great Britain can be very rough indeed. I had only been aboard for two days when the weather turned nasty, the deck under my feet was not still and as I turned and walked to the galley my stomach was heaving. The smell of the curry that was done at least three times a week hit me. I turned, bolted for the ships ablutions and was violently sick, then, feeling weak-kneed, attempted to do my job in the galley. For the next two days I battled against sea sickness – no-one gets any sympathy for this complaint you simply have to work your way through it. While it was happening to me I wondered, not for the first time, just what I had got myself into.

This was a seven day a week job and the rest of the crew were no help, 'Never mind nipper, all you need is a big fat greasy bacon sandwich.'

All of this work and sickness for the princely sum of £12 10s a month, of which £8 was sent home to my mother. Miraculously though I woke up on the third day feeling perfectly alright and also decidedly hungry. The seas around the ship were just as rough but I now had my sea legs under me.

We docked that same day, and after unloading headed back to Fawley. Empty, and thrown about more than ever, this didn't bother me at all. In fact from that day on, the rougher the sea the happier it made me. I was never seasick again, and it was this that prompted me to approach the chief steward to leave the ship. He asked me why and I told him I wanted to go deep sea to other countries. He said he understood this and made the necessary arrangements.

As I left for the last time I said goodbye to my fellow boy ratings. They had helped me settle into life in the Merchant Navy and I was grateful to them both. Two days later I was back at the Shipping Federation office and when it was my turn to be seen I was offered a saloon boy's job aboard the Union Castle liner *Winchester Castle*. I was over the moon and took the berth without any hesitation at all. These ships went to South Africa and my great adventure was about to start.

She wasn't the same size and class as the big Cunard ships, but she took my breath away. The *Winchester Castle* was due to sail on Thursday at four o'clock in the afternoon. I was joining on Monday which meant I had just three days to find my way around. There was a series of long alleyways leading in different directions, with hordes of crew members rushing about. I was lost in the melee until someone took pity on me.

'Just joining son? Right follow me.' I was led on a bewildering journey through the bowels of the ship, before coming out on deck at the stern end, where he left me with the man who looked after the catering crew's accommodation.

He was a kindly, but no nonsense man who took me to the cabins and ablutions. When I saw these I knew at once why the sea school training had been so strict. At the end of the alleyway were the ablutions, a large room with a line of sinks along one bulkhead. Facing these on the port side were showers and on the starboard side toilet cubicles. There would be no privacy here. The showers had no curtains or doors so were open to anyone passing by. These ablutions were used on a daily basis by everyone; dining saloon stewards, cabin stewards, bath stewards and all of the ship's boys.

On a ship this size there were more personnel in just the catering department than the entire crew of the one I had just left. He then took me to the boy ratings cabin where I would be sleeping. I was a little puzzled, this was the men's accommodation area but I could smell perfume. It was the kind of smell I associated with my days as Ted Martin's butcher's boy. His wife was very particular about her appearance and always wore perfume like this when she was in the shop, but why could I smell it here?

One cabin had its door open and I stopped dead. It was full of women, there were curtains up at the portholes and at least five of them were inside doing their hair and makeup. Why were they billeted here with the men?

'Keep away from that cabin,' I was told. 'They aren't women, they're men who dress like that, make sure you keep away from them.'

Trying to get over this I was shown into the saloon boy's cabin. It had double bunks along each bulkhead and accommodated twelve boys. Five of them were here and they gave me a warm greeting, showing me which of these bunks was mine. The next three days went by in a whirl of activity. The dining saloon was huge and we needed to learn where everything was kept, from table linen to condiments. We learnt the day-to-day routine of laying up tables, waiting on officers and guests, and balancing a tray on one hand while bringing it through the doors of the pantry flat. The meat was always on the plate ready and then vegetables were offered. These were on a platter and served by means of a large spoon and fork, held in one hand. I had done this time and time again on the *Vindi*, but being required to do it for real was a daunting prospect. I dropped more than I actually served but finally got the hang of it.

Because I lived in Southampton I was able to go home every night, but on Thursday morning I came on board ready for the voyage, where my companions greeted me, 'You think it's been busy in the saloon, wait till the bloods arrive today.'

Seeing my blank look they explained that 'bloods' were actually the passengers. From dinner on the first night out everyone would be allocated a table where they would sit for all their meals.

So at twelve o'clock I stood nervously at a table laid for fourteen people. At no time did I have that many to wait on, much to my relief, but what I did have was a continuous stream of passengers. After coming aboard and being shown their cabins they now came in search of lunch. It went on for just over three hours and I lost count of how many times I went in and out of the saloon bringing food to the table.

Once we got to the pantry flat for our own meal, I realised why the food at Sharpness had been so bad. It prepared us perfectly for eating what was left over and kept warm while the passengers' lunch was served. What we were given was quite frankly dreadful and I very quickly discovered Worcestershire sauce. No matter how bad the food, this was strong enough to disguise the awful taste.

We were so busy none of us noticed the ship slipping her moorings at four o'clock precisely, and making her way down Southampton water towards the open sea. We went below to our cabin for a well-earned rest before presenting ourselves in white jackets, freshly pressed black trousers and black shoes for the evening meal. This was very different from the bustle of lunch; passengers had now been allocated their regular tables. All the boy ratings had smaller tables to look after and I managed well that first night, getting better as the voyage continued.

Our first port of call was the lovely island of Madeira. We couldn't tie up here because they didn't have berthing facilities for a ship this size, so we anchored off and passengers were taken ashore by motor launch. There was no shore leave for the crew but I stood on deck and gazed in awe at this beautiful island rising steeply out of the sea. For the first time in my life I was looking at land that was not part of the country of my birth.

I bought a canary from one of the many traders who came on board, then we headed out into the Atlantic Ocean for a crossing that would take ten days to complete. This I enjoyed immensely. When not working I spent a lot of time on the poop deck at the stern of the ship taking in the sights. I never tired of watching albatross' swooping and skimming the wave tops, flying fish and occasionally whales and dolphins. If another vessel was sighted the excitement was felt all over the ship.

As this was my first crossing of the Atlantic I had one thing to worry about. We were approaching the equator and I had been told about the embarrassing things done to people at the crossing the line ceremony. To make matters worse I was the only new boy on this trip, which meant I would be the centre of attention. So I worked out a plan with the rest of the boys to hideout and not appear again until the next day. There were at least three full ratings on board who hadn't crossed before and they would be the ones to suffer.

So when this day came I wasn't worried. At lunch time all the boys were ready to go to the dining saloon as usual. It was suggested that as it was so hot we wouldn't go by the normal route but along deck, through the tourist passenger area. This was allowed, so I saw nothing wrong at all. We were dressed in our saloon uniforms and talking amiably together when we came alongside the passengers' swimming pool.

That's when the roof fell in on me. My mates had been through this ceremony before and it was a tradition, so their offer of help was just a blind. They had well and truly set me up. All I heard was the sudden shout of 'grab him' before being pounced on. They had hold of my arms and legs and as they moved to the side of the pool their intention became very clear. I did everything I could to prevent it by struggling and trying to free myself but to no avail.

Before I knew it they were swinging me back and forth until, on the count of three, I found myself airborne; landing with a huge splash I disappeared beneath the surface. Making it to the side of the pool I emerged, to the great amusement of the watching passengers, with water gushing out of my clothes. The rest of the saloon boys were laughing as uproariously as everyone else and I must have looked an absolute idiot.

With all this merriment ringing in my ears I sloshed my way back to our cabin to change. Embarrassing as it was, this experience meant I was now fully initiated and I really began to enjoy it from then on. Especially that night when the other three men were stripped, had all sorts of things squirted over their bodies and were paraded around from cabin to cabin. What happened to me was tame by comparison.

My first sight of South Africa was when we woke up to find the ship had docked during the early hours of the morning in Cape Town. As I went on deck I was struck by the splendour of Table Mountain, which dominated the skyline. It rose so majestically and it was the first time in my life I had seen any sort of mountain. Up to this moment I had only seen cliffs at various seaside resorts in the south of England. How a boy from Belgrave Road could end up visiting a place like this was beyond my understanding.

The atmosphere on board was more relaxed now, most of the passengers had disembarked during the day and I had been given a tip as a thank you for my services. We went ashore that night and for the first time in my life I set foot in another country. It was tempered somewhat by what I had seen aboard the ship during the day, and by what I could see now. Apartheid was in force in South Africa.

All through the day black men had been working on board. They were dressed in rags and starving, to the point where they were prepared to fight one another to get at the ship's many gash buckets that were filled with food we no longer required.

This was very apparent on shore too. Everything was labelled either 'European' or 'non-European', and it was necessary to get this right. Even the buses had this marked along with their destination number so we could only travel on the European ones. This was foreign to me, having been brought up in a very friendly place. To see people in their own country being treated as outcasts was very hard to take.

The trip around the coast was superb. Port Elizabeth, East London and the breathtaking beauty of Durban filled me with wonder. Then with a ship full of passengers we began the journey home. This time, after the ten-day Atlantic crossing, we stopped at Los Palmas, and managed to come alongside and enjoy a few hours ashore. Four days later I woke up and found the ship once more in Southampton Docks. I was paid off with the accumulated wages of six weeks, less the money I had sent home, and bought some apples, grapes and a sack of large juicy oranges for my family. I was still left with more money than I had ever had in my life before.

The taxi carried me into Belgrave Road and I gave the now familiar direction to the driver, 'The next lamp post on the right please.' Then it was up the short garden path into the house where my mother was waiting to throw her arms around me and welcome me home. I did this on four more occasions, each time enjoying two weeks leave before rejoining the *Winchester Castle* and setting out on the Cape-run again.

The fifth time, however, I realised I wanted something different from this routine. Waiting on tables was not supposed to be done by the ship's boy ratings, but each of us did it every time. After each meal we then had to do our own job, cleaning the dining saloon and making sure everything was put away properly. It was a tough life and didn't give us much time to ourselves, so I made it known among my cabin mates that this would be my last trip. They were disappointed because we had all become close friends, but they saw I was serious and wished me luck on whichever ship I was signed onto next. However, the *Winchester Castle* had not finished with me yet and managed to leave a legacy that has stayed with me.

On the return trip when the ship was once again alongside the quay in Cape Town, my mates told me I wouldn't be going ashore with them tonight. Instead I would be going out with some of the ship's stewards. This was so unusual so I just gaped at them. 'It's your birthday and they're taking you out,' they said. The date was 6 December 1957 and I had just reached the age of seventeen.

The evening began with a visit to the theatre, where the British comedian Tommy Trinder was the star turn. The only one I had been in up until now was the Grand Theatre in Southampton. But that was no comparison to this huge and lavish place of entertainment. To sit here and laugh at a famous English comedian made it much more enjoyable. After the show I was smuggled into Cape Town's premier night club, Del Monicos. Here I was treated to Cape brandy and took to it like a duck to water. Brandy taken without any additives such as water or ginger ale is one of life's pleasures that I have enjoyed on numerous occasions.

The floor show that night was wonderful and the highlight was the performance of a young woman who was totally magic on the electric organ. Her name was Cherry Wainer. There was nothing she couldn't do and the audience received her act with booming applause. In the early sixties she came to England and made a name for herself here as well. As we left the club I thanked everybody for giving me such a good time. But as the night air hit me, the brandy started to take effect and I was decidedly wobbly on my legs.

I lost consciousness long before I got back to the ship and was carried below and put to bed by the stewards. Next morning I woke up to find that death was probably much better than the way I was feeling. I had a hangover and it was much worse than anything I had previous suffered. But we were on board a ship and it was necessary for me to serve breakfast as usual.

I don't know how I got through that meal, but the passengers at my table received the service they expected and all were fed properly. The food was making my stomach heave and the stewards who had taken me out were enjoying this as they knew it was the start of a bad few days. Cape brandy is notorious for having an awful effect and I found this out very quickly. Even when you start to feel better, the moment you drink any sort of liquid the hang over comes back and you feel as bad as before.

While in Cape Town, I received a letter telling me the Marsh family had joined the growing number of working class households that now had television. Having been brought up thus far on radio this was a revelation. I came into the house just before Christmas, after that last trip on the *Winchester Castle,* to see the 17-inch black and white set proudly placed on top of the sideboard. With just BBC programmes available, my mother switched off the radio at five o'clock every day and turned the television on.

The age of the rented television had arrived and for my mother this was a giant step forward. She had been devoted to the radio for many years but always went to the cinema once a week. It made no difference at all what film was showing, Thursday was plainly and simply her cinema night. Now she could watch films, as well as serials and quiz shows, from the comfort of her own home, an unbelievable luxury.

In those early days the rental company also supplied the aerial that went on the roof. All was well until dad lost his job and for a time money was too tight to keep up the payments each week. Dad soon got back into work, but not before the TV was taken back, and our mother had to sit in deep gloom every evening, just looking at the space where our set had stood. This situation changed when dad got another set. My mother's world had been set to rights, once more a television sat on top of the sideboard and she could enjoy the benefit of the programmes. A few days later there was a loud knock on the front door. Opening it mum was confronted by two very burly men, 'Evening Missis, we're from the TV rental company and we've come to take the aerial back.' My mother is a very small woman and these men towered over her, but as their words sank in, she realised if they went ahead she would be left with a TV that would show no pictures at all.

'What did you say? You're going to take my aerial, over my dead body you are, get away from my house and don't come back.'

'Listen Missis,' the biggest of the men said, 'we've been told to reclaim this aerial and that's what we're going to do.'

Small she may be, but threaten to take away either her radio or her television and you really are asking for trouble. 'Get out,' she yelled, giving the nearest of these men a hefty push that sent him cannoning into his mate who was standing just behind him. 'Get away from my house, go on get out.'

'Now listen, we've got our orders and you shouldn't be treating us like this'.

My mother, now a small bundle of fury, ran at them and the last thing I remember was those workmen saying, 'Bloody hell, let's get out of here', as they were chased back into their van by my very diminutive mother, then nearly broke the speed limit racing away. That aerial eventually came down, but not until the rest of the house did as well.

As for me it was now time to apply for my next berth and, after turning down the chance to join two more Union Castle Liners, I was offered the job of pantry boy on a tanker, the *Ruth Lake*. She was new, built by Swan Hunter & Wigham Richardson Ltd in 1956. When I joined her she was operating as a tanker for the Esso Company, and I noticed at once she didn't have the traditional cat walk over her deck used by crew members who needed to get from the stern to the centre castle in any sort of weather.

I was received on board and shown the boy ratings cabin by a Scotsman who was the second steward. I had just come from a passenger liner where twelve boys were housed in very primitive conditions. Now I was in a room with just three occupants, two bunks on one side and one on the other. What was next to this single bunk, which incidentally quickly became mine, left me absolutely dumb struck. It was our own private ablutions.

They say the *Titanic* was the ship of dreams, but to me so was the *Ruth Lake*. She was only used as a tanker during the winter months in Canada, where it got so cold that mining was impossible. However as soon as spring arrived she reverted to her main function as an iron-ore carrier, operated by the transport company of Canada Ltd. She needed to have her tanks in open space with nothing in the way because the ore came straight off a conveyor then off at the other end in the United States.

This answered my question about the missing catwalk. The way to get to the centre castle and back in bad weather was shown to me and the other boy who would be working the pantry amidships. At the end of the crew's alleyway, on both the port and starboard side, were hatchways leading down to tunnels. These ran alongside the ships tanks below deck, through a series of watertight doors, before coming out inside the centre castle. Both of us got to know these tunnels very well indeed along with the huge boom on the deck above as the sea crashed inboard.

We had one trip to the Middle East for a cargo of oil. This took six weeks and was long enough to get to know the ship and crew I would be living among. The ship's cook was a real character, known as 'Doc'. He wore plimsolls with no laces, no socks, scruffy jeans and tops that would have been turned down if offered to a charity. The food he turned out was quite simply out of this world. The second steward became more of a friend than a boss, although we still couldn't get away with anything.

Every day I cleaned and dusted the engineers' lounge, then it was down to the pantry to get ready for breakfast. For this meal I was responsible for the toast and boiled eggs and got to know all the officers' preferences. From the captain down, I knew who liked their toast lightly or well done, and who wanted runny eggs or hard boiled. Brian, my fellow pantry boy, and I relieved each other for our meals.

After breakfast one of my jobs was to get coffee to the engineers on watch. The simple way was to put a tray with coffee and a selection of biscuits into the engineer lift and send it down. I, however, elected to take it myself and took the tray, balancing it on one hand, through the engine-room escape hatch. I then had to negotiate a series of ladders that led me down onto the boiler flat. Once there I said a chirpy good morning to the firemen on duty before going on through into the engine room up to the starting platform. To be in a ship's engine room at sea has to be experienced. The noise is unbelievable and not once was I able to make myself heard. If I needed to say anything it was done by sign language.

Arriving back with a full load of oil from the Middle East, we came into Fawley to unload. I had one night at home then had to be back on board for the trip across to Holland. Here the ship went into dry dock to be converted from an oil to an iron-ore carrier. Most of the crew went home while this was being done, then, three weeks later, rejoined in Rotterdam. After taking on stores we made the Atlantic crossing that would take us first to the iron-ore mining town of Sept-Iles. This is on the St Lawrence River in Quebec. We would be coming in and out of this French-Canadian port for the next six months, taking on full loads of iron ore and shipping it to either Philadelphia or Baltimore.

Sept-Iles was a small town that reminded me so much of the cowboy films I had grown-up with. It could only be described as a one-horse town and had board-walks instead of pavements. Since we were still only boys, getting into bars was out of the question. Twenty-one was the legal age here, as well as in the United States, and we were never going to be able to prove we were that age. So we went to the cinema instead. There were two of these in town, one showing an English film and the other French, so our choice was made easy.

In the USA things were different; there were so many places to see and things to do. In Philadelphia for instance a gent's outfitter came on board. As soon as any of us came on deck he would point and shout, 'Hey I got a shirt for you', the word shirt in his broad American accent sounding like 'shoit'. They were good shirts though and we always bought some. I had the time of my life going up and down the American coast that year, never being in port for more than two days before putting to sea again.

The chief steward was a man we had to be wary of because he was a strict disciplinarian and also the ship's first aid officer; I needed his help on one very memorable occasion. We were at sea on a reasonably calm day when I had to go forward to the mid-ship's pantry. There was a bit of a swell but nothing to worry about. We were fully loaded so very low in the water, but the sun was shining and I was enjoying the air as I walked along the deck.

I reached the pantry, collected whatever I needed, had a chat with Brian then made my way aft again. I was roughly three-quarters of the way back along the deck when a boom, the like of which I had heard many times before – from the safety of the tunnel – sounded behind me. I knew at once what this meant; we had taken water and it was rushing towards me.

One of the things we had been taught during our *Vindi* training was, should you find yourself in this position, grab the nearest solid object and hang on. The water will pass over and all you will suffer is a soaking. Sound advice and there were plenty of things in easy reach to accomplish this; but, the companion-way, leading to the upper deck and safety, was tantalisingly near, and I made the near fatal mistake of thinking I could reach it in time.

Starting to run I found myself swamped by an inrush of water. It went over my head and lifted me off the deck until I was hurled up against the aft-bulkhead. Fortunately for me the ship had heeled to starboard and I was thrown inboard. Had she gone to port I could so easily have been swept over the side. As it was, I was left choking on the sea water I had swallowed, and all the breath had been knocked out of my body by the ferocity of that wave.

I managed to crawl to the companionway and got halfway up before collapsing in an undignified heap. I heard shouts above me then my arms were grasped and I was pulled the rest of the way to safety. Carried swiftly down to the boys' cabin my wet clothes were stripped off and I was put into my bunk. The chief steward was quickly in attendance but I couldn't explain what had happened. Shock had set in and my teeth were clattering together. I had to stay in my bunk for the next twenty-four hours, being closely watched all the time, before coming back to normal.

Before returning to duty I got a well-deserved lecture from my senior officer. He asked me where I should have been when going from the stern to the centre castle in even the slightest of swells.

'In the tunnel, sir.'

'Yes,' he said, 'but you weren't were you? You were on deck.'

'Yes sir,' I replied sheepishly.

He then drilled the point home:

How do you think the captain would have explained the loss of one of the youngest members of his crew? Make no mistake about it, had you gone over the side we would have had little or no chance of finding you. This is a big ship, it takes time to turn, and you're not exactly big are you? Then it would have been my job to try and explain to your parents how we lost their son overboard. In future Marsh, think before you act.

The fact he referred to me as this, instead of my shipboard nick-name of Jasper, was proof enough of how annoyed he was and he was right to be, I should have known better.

November of that memorable year saw us at Sept-Iles for the last time; walking into the town it was obvious this would be the case. The Canadian winter had taken hold, we were walking through deep snow, and it was freezing. We left for Philadelphia and after unloading made our way round to Brooklyn to go into dry dock. This was so the ship could be converted once again to carrying oil. As this would take at least three weeks to complete, we had a very good time here.

Brian and I were surprised when after breakfast on the second day we were told we could have the rest of the day off. We lost no time changing and were soon in a taxi heading across the Brooklyn Bridge into Manhattan. Our first stop was to visit what was then the world's largest structure, the Empire State building. I may not have a head for heights but the view from the top of that building was outstanding. We were typical tourists, going everywhere of interest, and in the evening went to Times Square cinema before returning to the ship.

Brian and I found everything about New York so fascinating. We went ashore each night and it was a time, I'm sure, he remembers with as much pleasure as I do. Those three weeks in dry dock simply flew past and when the job was complete we went ashore for the last time, having spent most of the day provisioning the ship. We made the most of the last night coming back later than usual. The next day, during a heavy snow fall, the *Ruth Lake* made her way out to sea and I stood at the stern watching New York fade away into the distance.

We were bound for Venezuela in South America to take on a full cargo of oil. In just two or three days we went from bitter cold to tropical heat. Our destination was an oil depot and that was all there was to see. We were given shore leave, but issued with passes and told not to lose them because we would not be allowed back into the depot without them. This we believed because as we walked towards the exit we were watched all the way by rifle-toting guards. After an evening spent in an old shack that served as a bar, we went back aboard to prepare for the Atlantic crossing that would end at Fawley oil refinery.

The homeward trip began in late November so after just a week my birthday came round. There would be nothing like last year's surprise in South Africa. We were at sea and birthdays were not acknowledged, so on the morning of 6 December 1958 I went to work as usual. Dinner had been served and I was preparing the pantry for the next day's breakfast. Suddenly the chief steward came in and by the look on his face, I could see he wasn't very happy. To say I was surprised is an understatement; at this time of the day he should be in the bonded store, handing out the regular two bottles of beer to all of the ship's ratings and two bottles of Pepsi to each of the three boys. So what was he doing here?

He glared at me. 'Have you cleaned the engineers' rest room today?'

I just stared back and stuttered, 'Yes sir.'

'Then why is it in such a bad state? I've just been up there and it's filthy, go and clean it at once. I will be inspecting it again so make sure there is nothing for me to find.'

With that he disappeared making his way to the bonded store and I was dumbstruck. I was just going off duty but would have to go and clean a room I had already done that morning.

I looked at the second steward but all I got was, 'I don't know, but you better get on with it – that was a direct order.' So, with a huge amount of bad grace I got all the cleaning materials together and went back up to the engineer's rest room. I was fuming with rage because this wasn't fair. I did this each morning and never had a complaint before. What's more I could see nothing wrong with it now, so what was the chief steward talking about when he said it was filthy?

But an order is an order and I cleaned all the surfaces again, including the deck. Then, putting the cleaning materials away, I made my way back through the deserted galley and crew's mess to the boy-ratings cabin. Opening the door I found most of the ship's company, a loud shout of 'Happy Birthday' went up, and I was mobbed. The cabin had been decorated and filled with food and drink and I couldn't find anything to say, beyond thank you. I couldn't believe they had gone to so much trouble and the reason was I was now eighteen, and would be taken on my next ship as a full rating. Twenty-one was the coming of age ashore, but at sea this was the equivalent.

I was still coming to terms with this when I was reminded the chief steward was in the bonded store waiting for me so I hurried down. Nothing was said apart from my asking for 'two bottles of Pepsi please'. He disappeared into the store and came back with two bottles which he placed in front of me. They weren't Pepsi however, but beer. I looked from them to him and he smiled and said 'Happy Birthday'. I smiled back and said 'Thank you.' This meant so much to me, all my shipmates were congratulating me and telling me I had grown-up. It turned out to be a wonderful night and set up the rest of the journey home.

Arriving back at Fawley left me with very mixed emotions. It was great to be back in the UK again after such a long trip and I was eager once again to see my home. But I would have to say goodbye to this ship that had come to mean so much to me. I would not be able to rejoin her because the two stewards were staying aboard and the boy's job I had been doing would now be offered to the next boy rating applying for a berth.

I arrived home to a rapturous welcome and had a very memorable Christmas. Southampton's High Street was lit up with lights and at home in Belgrave Road we had a tree for the first time. Standing proudly in the front room window, its lights shone into the dark outside and it looked wonderful. My brother reminded me that Christmas Day this year, 1958, marked the 25th anniversary of my parent's wedding. So to celebrate this milestone I joined my brother and sisters and contributed to the one thing we knew would give our mother so much pleasure. We bought her a carpet for the front room and secretly had it laid while we were all out enjoying Christmas Eve. Her delight when she saw it will live with us all for a very long time. No more time spent polishing the lino, and we all agreed it couldn't have happened to a more deserving person.

After that memorable Christmas I went again to the Shipping Federation and was offered a full ratings job aboard the *Arundel Castle*. I wasn't over the moon because I didn't really want the Cape-run again. I was told, however, I would only need to do one trip on her to get my rate then I could choose whatever line I wanted to serve with. For me this meant tankers because I had started a love affair with these ships and wanted to get back aboard one as quickly as possible.

The rest of that year and well into the next wasn't a huge success. Every time I came back I was offered nothing but Union Castle liners, and took the jobs even though I was now thoroughly fed up with the sight of Cape Town. It ended inevitably with a huge row at the Shipping Federation offices. This didn't go down well and finally finished my career. The Merchant Navy had already started to dwindle and I could see the end was in sight for this mighty fleet as far as British crews were concerned.

I had enjoyed my time so much but now it was over. I needed a new direction, and quickly. I knew I couldn't settle to life in a factory after the past few adventurous years, so looked around in earnest for something that would present me with a challenge, and suddenly found the answer had been staring me in the face. Living close to the London to Bournemouth Railway line I had taken trains for granted, much as I had done with the famous liners before deciding to try my luck at joining them. So why not do it again? After all it is every boy's dream of becoming a train driver so why not find out if there is a chance of getting a job as a railway fireman?

The thought had no sooner entered my head than I decided to act on it. In so doing I began another career on the footplate of Britain's steam railway. This too was heading for decline as diesel and electric power were poised to take over. Still, there was enough left for me to enjoy at least five years at this exciting job working from the railway yards at Eastleigh. There were many things that happened during those heady days but that, as they say, is another story.

Fate soon took over and gave me something else to worry about. The road where I had spent all my life had for some time been under threat. The German Luftwaffe had not been able to touch it during the war but it was now in much more danger from Southampton City Council. We had been hearing rumours for a number of months that Belgrave Road was to be demolished to make room for a new bypass.

12

# Late of Belgrave Road

By the time the axe landed on Belgrave Road most of my family had married or simply just moved away. Still it left us feeling just as empty when we found out the awful rumours about the bypass were true. My parents, who had lived in this wonderful house for well over thirty years and raised a family of six here, had to start packing their possessions and prepare for a move they certainly didn't want to make. My elder sisters and my brother George were frequent visitors during this time.

On one occasion, while all this disruption was going on, I stood in the long back garden and relived some of the happy memories of my childhood, the outside toilet with the door that had never been fitted with a lock, the back door itself with broken wood at the bottom of the glass panels. In all the time I lived here this was always how the door looked. Those panels were never repaired. Neither was the long crack in the drainpipe which carried water off the roof, or the broken concrete of the back steps.

The patch in the centre of the garden never produced vegetables of the same quality as the other parts. This was because every year on bonfire night my father supervised the fire we built, topped off by the Marriot's guy. This part of the garden should have received extra fertilization to combat the ashes that were always left, but it never got any, the ashes were simply dug into the ground. In fact my father never used fertilizer at all, but horse manure – that was now collected by Ron and Jean. When he first started to dig and plant this very long garden he got the most amazing results: huge potatoes, along with carrots, cabbages, peas, and delicious runner beans. But as year followed year the produce got smaller and smaller.

My two elder sisters and my brother had moved out to homes of their own. Dad was away more than ever now, going all over the country in his job as a foreman steel-erector. So the job of doing the garden fell to me. I had the help of our next-door neighbour, whose own garden was so well kept. This was another feature of this friendly road; I knew nothing about gardening, but with his help I managed to get the soil ready for planting. I had a measure of success, though I was surprised when Ron and Jean charged me a shilling for the manure. Inflation was starting to rear its head – we only got sixpence a bucket when we were collecting and selling. I didn't tackle the big job of potato planting but managed everything else, including a good salad crop.

In other ways our neighbour came to my aid, often without being asked. This was very apparent when the back garden gate, which had been rotting away for a number of years, finally gave up the struggle and collapsed on top of the dustman. To say he wasn't pleased is something of an understatement. The gist of it was that, unless we repaired the gate by next week neither he nor any of his workmates would come into our garden to empty the bin.

This was serious so something clearly had to be done. I inspected the damage the next day and discovered that a new gate post was needed, the old one having rotted right through. So I looked in the shed and found what I thought would be alright for the job. A wooden post dad had brought home some years ago and never used was the right size. This was the answer to my problem.

All I had to do now was dig out the old post, enlarge the hole and place the new one into it. Then I would fasten the hinges of the gate and the whole thing would be as good as new. It was as I started to dig the hole I found it wasn't going to be as easy as I imagined. I was sweating profusely and quite frankly getting nowhere when the gentle voice of Mr Childs, my neighbour, interrupted me, 'What are you trying to do Jimmy?'

When I told him he looked and simply shook his head. 'This won't do at all. The post isn't anywhere near strong enough to support a gate of this size. And you'll need a deeper hole with plenty of rubble for extra strength, hold on a moment.'

With this he went back into his own garden and returned shortly with a very much better post and a large quantity of concrete. For the next two hours he dug out the hole and placed the post in it, then fortified the whole thing. As I watched him I knew without any doubt this job was beyond my limited capabilities. So did Mr Childs, and as he knew my father was away and I was the only one available to do the job he took over and did it for me. This was just another example of the sort of life we all knew in Belgrave Road.

We in turn helped them every year when they went away on holiday. They had a superbly trained dog called Rex who never at any time strayed into our garden, always keeping to his own as he had been taught. But for those two weeks the Childs family was away he came and stayed with us. We loved it when he was there, he was such a well-behaved dog, but our cats, Blitz and Timmy, were most put out. He stayed with us in our house and garden and never crossed the fence at all. But the moment his own family returned he gave a joyful bark and leapt over the fence to be reunited with them.

The house had so many memories for me. The front room was always kept as a show room throughout the year but lit up like a fairy grotto at Christmas. Nobody was allowed in this hallowed room during the year but if anyone, either related directly to the family or close friends, were in trouble with accommodation, mum would immediately offer them the use of this room. Over the years more than one couple started their married life there. As did at least two families, both with children, until suitable housing could be found for them.

As I stood in the garden that day I looked at the spot where the old shed had stood for so many years, defying the elements and avoiding complete collapse. It leaned over a bit more with each passing year, yet never at any time did it actually fall. In there had been the wood and accessories needed for our orange-box racers and later our bikes. All of dad's gardening tools were kept there as well as everything else a family accumulates.

In those times a lock was not even thought of as being needed, which was just as well because this shed didn't have a door. Despite this nothing was ever stolen. We had no reason to think any of our neighbours would steal from us and we wouldn't do it to them. Indeed my mother always kept the key to our house in the front-door lock, so that when any of us came home all we had to do was turn the key and open the door. Mrs Childs from next door often did this if she needed to see mum, in any context, and this too was normal routine.

Ron and Jean knew this era of Belgrave Road better than we did as they grew up a long way behind Sue, Pat, George and me. Both still lived at home, but Ron, by now, was planning to marry his girlfriend Valerie. She had stayed with us a year before at Christmas and had enjoyed it so much because of the way my mother always welcomed visitors. Every Boxing Day one of George's friends came over, as his family spent that day with relatives he didn't like. The alternative for him was to be embraced in the warmth and friendliness of our home, surely all of this couldn't just come to an end?

Sadly, in late 1968, I stood outside a now empty No.94 and looked at what was left of a life I had known so well for at least twenty-eight years. The front door was hanging open and the small hall beyond where George and I had played endless games in our youth was now an empty, neglected space. This was always our first sight of home and meant so much every time I returned from one of my trips to sea.

As I stood with a lump in my throat a familiar voice sounded behind me.

'Come to have a last look Jim?'

I spun round and saw Mr Whelan standing there. 'Yes, I still can't believe it's happened.'

'Neither can any of us,' he said, 'but it has so we have to pick up the pieces and move on.' This of course was true but for many who had lived their lives here this was impossible to accept. In one case an elderly lady kept coming back even though all her furniture had been moved into a flat. She just sat in her old house that now had no gas or electricity because she couldn't bear to leave it. This came to an end when the bulldozers finally rolled and demolished every house.

On the last day my family lived at No.94 my two sisters were there to give all the help they could. With the furniture out and on its way to the new address, they were stunned when mum appeared, carrying a bucket of soapy water.

'What are you going to do with that?' they both demanded.

'The windows are dirty, I must give them a clean, I can't have my windows looking like that'.

Well the front room had always been mum's show room and we were never allowed there during the year, but to want to clean them now?

'Mum,' Sue said, 'the Cranes and bulldozers are already here, they're going to knock the houses down in the next few days. What possible difference can it make if the windows have got a bit of dust on them, they're going to be smashed to pieces aren't they?'

'I can't help that,' mum said, vigorously applying her cloth full of Sunlight soap suds over the big panes of glass. 'No-one will say my house wasn't presentable at anytime while I have lived here.'

Just a few days later the home of my birth went the same way as the rest of the houses, as those wrecking cranes and bulldozers did their work. My mother's windows glowed right up until the moment that massive iron globe swung through the air and smashed them into very small splinters

Ironically the bypass that sounded the death knell for Belgrave Road never went through it. It was built behind the road where we all grew up, and that happy place now exists as an industrial estate. Gone are the laughter and tears of generations of Belgrave dwellers, and in their place are warehouses.

Although the houses are gone, the road itself will never die. So many of the wonderful friends I grew up with are still in touch with one another. I met up with them all as the twenty-first century began. We met in one of Southampton's hotels and the clock turned back to the days of our childhood. Sadly some of our numbers were depleted, Victor Warrender having tragically died of a heart attack some years before. But most of the old crowd was there and the girls were represented by Dianne Cope and Vickie Masterman, both no longer known by those surnames of course because they had been married for a number of years. Also there were Dave Simmonds and Bobby Westmore with their wives. Edwin Whelan joined us as well and looked no different from when I had last seen him. And to my delight Pat Marriot was there with his wife.

Pat had gone from Belgrave Road and I lost touch with him from the time I left the timber yard in Southampton Docks to go to sea school in 1957. Since then he had married and he and his wife brought up their family in a beautiful house he had built for them in the rural setting of the New Forest. It was very fortunate that I met him again because I soon found out he was suffering from cancer. He hadn't changed in character in all the years since I had last seen him. His outlook on life was to live it to the full and enjoy it, so, even though this awful illness was gripping him, the Pat Marriot indomitable spirit still proudly stood out.

That night in the hotel I told him the only change I could see in him from the times when we ran the streets in and around our road was the colour of his hair. Pat and I met once more after that and, as we sat together, inevitably started to talk of those halcyon days of our childhood. I will always remember how much he laughed as we recalled one calamity after another, most of which were instigated by him. That was the kind of person he was, never challenging us to anything he wasn't prepared to do himself. He, I truly believe, was the real spirit of Belgrave Road.

I was always proud that I got through the tough course at the *Vindicatrix* Sea-Training School and swell with pride when I say to anyone I am a Vindi boy. Yet I never forget that I am even more proud to say I am a Belgrave boy. These words that sum up what it means to have been brought up in so wonderful a road.

Now, although the former residents are scattered around the city of Southampton, the love of it still links us all together. When a death does occur there is a poignant statement made in reference to the person in Southampton's local newspaper. The name appears and next to it, 'late of Belgrave road'. It is something we all understand and it means such a lot to every one of us who still survive; the road itself will never die. The houses may be gone and the road reduced to nothing, but while just one of us who lived there still draws breath Belgrave Road lives on through us. Even when we are all gone, the children we have raised will remember the road their parents were so proud of, and will undoubtedly tell their own children the stories that have been handed down to them.

When my time comes to exit this world, I know that next to my name in the obituary column will be those immortal words so proudly earned. The statement will read, 'James Marsh ... Late of Belgrave Road.'

# Bibliography

Websites:

www.dyerbros.co.uk
www.forestprints.co.uk/sharpness.htm
www.johnfhunt.co.uk
www.pennylegg.com
www.stdenysboats.co.uk
www.vindicatrix-hq.fsnet.co.uk
www.woodmill.co.uk
http://buddyboard.writingbuddies.net
www.whitenap.plus.com/itchen/


Other:

Documents and maps of Belgrave Road, by permission of Southampton Archives.

# Other titles published by The History Press

## Southampton: Gateway to the World
ALASTAIR ARNOTT

The history of Southampton is tied to its maritime heritage. This book explores the intimate relationship the city has with its near neighbour the sea, tracing its development throughout the centuries. *Southampton: A Gateway to the World* delves into the past of this thriving coastal city and discovers what events have taken place Written by a former Southampton museum curator, this bo provides expert insight into the history of shipping, traditionally the city's most prominent industry

978 0 7524 5357 6

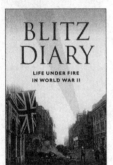

## Blitz Diary: Life Under Fire in the Second World War
CAROL HARRIS

In *Blitz Diary* historian Carol Harris has collected together a remarkable series of accounts from the war's darkest days, with heart-warming stories of survival, perseverance, solidarity anc bravery, the preservation of which becomes increasingly important as the Blitz fades from livin memory. Harris tells the story of aerial attacks on Britain during the Second World War, throu the letters, diaries and memoirs of those who experienced it at first hand.

978 0 7524 5172 5

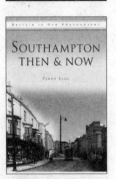

## Southampton Then & Now
PENNY LEGG

The major port city of Southampton has a rich heritage which is uniquely reflected in this fascinating new compilation. Contrasting a rare selection of archive images with full-colour modern photographs, this book reveals the ever-changing faces and buildings of Southampton Covering local landmarks, pubs and hotels, churches, parks, transport, work and leisure, this is a wide-ranging look at the city's colourful history.

978 0 7524 5693 5

## Haunted Southampton
PENNY LEGG

Explore the darkest secrets of Southampton's past with this collection of stories telling of the inexplicable occurrences and ghostly apparitions that have haunted the city for centuries. No matter where you are in the city, incidents of unexplained phenomena have taken place nearb Southampton is 'alive' with ghosts and, for those who dare, their stories can be discovered in t chilling book.

978 0 7524 5519 8

Visit our website and discover thousands of other History Press books.

**www.thehistorypress.co.uk**